AUSTRALIANS AT WAR

WAR AGAINST JAPAN
1942-1945

PETER CHARLTON

TIME-LIFE BOOKS. AUSTRALIA
in association with JOHN FERGUSON. SYDNEY

Designed and produced by
John Ferguson Pty Ltd
100 Kippax Street,
Surry Hills, NSW 2010

Series Editor: John Ferguson
Consulting Editor: George G. Daniels
Series Director: Lesley McKay
Editor: Tony Love
Picture Editor/Staff Writer: Julian Leatherdale
Designer: Jane Tenney
Production Manager: Tracy O'Shaughnessy
Picture Researchers: Julian Leatherdale, Tracy O'Shaughnessy
Production Assistant: Jo Taylor
Assembly Artists: Josie Howlett, Megan Smith

Time-Life Books, South Pacific Books Division
Managing Director: Bonita L. Boezeman
Production Manager: Ken G. Hiley
Production Assistant: Dimity Raftos

The Author: PETER CHARLTON is a
journalist, author and infantry officer in the
Australian Army Reserve. He has written
three books on military themes: *The Thirty-
Niners,* the story of the original volunteers
for the 2nd AIF; *The Unnecessary War,* an
account of the 1944-1945 island campaigns
of the Pacific War; and *Pozieres 1916,* which
described the World War I battle which
claimed as many Australian lives in five
weeks as the Pacific War took in five years.
He has also published a best-selling account
of Queensland politics, *State of Mind,* and a
history of the Australian passion for
gambling, *Two Flies Up A Wall.* He is the
associate editor of *The Courier Mail,*
Brisbane. He lives there with his wife and
two children. Charlton wrote *War Against
Japan 1941-1942,* another book in this series.

First published in 1989 by
Time-Life Books (Australia) Pty Ltd
15 Blue Street
North Sydney, NSW 2060.

National Library of Australia
cataloguing-in-publication data

Charlton, Peter, 1946-
    War Against Japan 1942-1945
    Bibliography.
    Includes index.
    ISBN 0 949118 27 3

1. World War, 1939-1945 — Campaigns — Pacific Area.
2. World War, 1939-1945 — Australia.
I. Title (Series: Australians at war; 11).
940.54'26

This publication has been partially funded by the Australian
Bicentennial Authority as part of its program to help
celebrate Australia's Bicentennial in 1988.

Printed in Hong Kong.

WAR AGAINST JAPAN
1942-1945

Kneeling beside a crude grave dug for 11 Japanese dead and marked by their steel helmets, young soldiers of Australia's 25th Brigade record a hard-won victory after vicious fighting on the Kokoda Trail around Gorari village in November 1942. The Australians in New Guinea fought more than one unremitting enemy: as well as the Japanese, they faced a merciless climate and terrain.

Australia
1788-1988

©

CONTENTS

1

STRUGGLE FOR PAPUA

As Japan's troops advanced on Port Moresby, Australia's beleaguered soldiers fought a costly retreat across the rugged Kokoda Trail. But the Diggers halted the enemy onslaught and were reinforced before fiercely pursuing the Japanese back to their northern bases.

George Allen's concrete sculpture "Papuan Native Carrier" pays tribute to the overworked porters on the Kokoda Trail.

By mid-1942 the balance of the Pacific War had swung in favour of the Allies. Despite the fall of Singapore, and Japan's capture of the ring of islands to the north of Australia, there had been strategic and psychological successes for the United States of America and Australia — at the Battle of the Coral Sea in early May, where the Japanese were turned back from an amphibious invasion of Port Moresby, and then at Midway in the North Pacific, where the might of Nippon's Navy was defeated and Japan's advantage at sea was checked.

These events offered the commander of the South West Pacific Area (SWPA), the American General Douglas MacArthur, an opportunity to move onto the offensive for the very first time in the war. But his preparations for such a move were affected by a "Beat Germany First" policy that British Prime Minister Winston Churchill and U.S. President Franklin D. Roosevelt had adopted at a meeting the previous Christmas. Roosevelt and America's senior strategists, the Joint Chiefs of Staff, were readying themselves for an invasion of Western Europe, then timed for the northern spring of 1943. There were few resources for MacArthur's planned Pacific operations, which included the capture of Japan's base at Rabaul, the occupation of the Solomons, and the seizure of Lae, Salamaua and the rest of New Guinea's north coast which the Japanese had taken in March to facilitate their bombing of Port Moresby.

Allied plans from there were to make further moves northwards, either to Malaya or more likely to the Philippines, and then hopefully on to Japan's home islands themselves. The Allies, however, needed airfields before any such offensive could take place, and construction was under way on Australia's Cape York Peninsula, at Port Moresby, and at Milne Bay in eastern New Guinea. It was hoped also to secure the Buna region on New Guinea's northeast coast to build further airstrips for bomber and fighter support of moves against Rabaul, New Britain, and New Ireland.

As part of the Allied presence in the region, a mixed force of commandos and a unit of resident Europeans in New Guinea, the New Guinea Volunteer Rifles, patrolled around Lae and Salamaua in an effort to keep the enemy on the coast. As well, the commander of Papua and New Guinea, Major General B.M. Morris, sent the 39th Battalion and a native unit led by Australian officers and NCOs, the Papuan Infantry Battalion, and some medical and service personnel into the hills; their job was to prevent the Japanese coming over the Owen Stanley Range, and to deal with any airborne landings along the Kokoda Trail. By mid-July 1942 "Maroubra Force", as Morris had called this group, was strung out between Ilolo, just north of Port Moresby, and Awala on the far side of the mountains, and the Australian 7th Brigade was stationed at Milne Bay, and America's Admiral Ernest J. King was preparing his Marine Corps to land on Guadalcanal in the Solomon Islands.

But the Japanese still dictated play around the northeast coast of New Guinea. With their plans to make an amphibious assault on Port Moresby forestalled after the naval setbacks of the previous months, the Japanese decided to go overland, across the rugged Owen Stanley Range, blindly hopeful that they could take New Guinea's major settlement and port in a few weeks.

And so, in July and August, the Japanese landed 13,500 troops near Buna and Gona, the first of them coming ashore at Basabua on July 21. They pushed quickly inland, forcing the forward companies of Papuans and the 39th Battalion back over the Kumusi River, which raced wildly down the eastern side of the ranges. The Australians, vastly outnumbered and totally unprepared, staged a fighting withdrawal all the way to Kokoda village, where they engaged the Japanese in close combat before pulling back once again, this time south to Deniki. Its food and ammunition severely depleted, and after an attempt to retake Kokoda was turned back even with one company of the 39th dug in at the village, Maroubra Force finally withdrew to Isurava, eight kilometres south of Deniki. The Japanese had now secured the Kokoda plateau and airfield, their staging post for a continuing assault on Port Moresby.

Even before the news of such reverses in the Owen Stanleys had reached Australia, the state of the fighting in Papua had convinced General MacArthur to reinforce Port Moresby. His original idea was to send in the U.S. 32nd Division, but this would have created immense practical difficulties: two formations, one Australian and one American, would then be operating in the same area but reporting to two headquarters still back in Australia. The Commander-in-Chief of Australian Military Forces, General Sir Thomas Blamey, convinced MacArthur that it would be preferable to give the responsibility of defending Port Moresby, and ultimately the counter-attack on the Japanese, to the Australians.

The 53rd Battalion, which had been part of the original Port Moresby garrison in 1941, was the first to go forward to join the 39th in the mountains. And more troops were on their way to New Guinea, from the AIF's 7th Division —

The Japanese had conquered most of the southwest Pacific by mid-1942, when they began their New Guinea offensive. Their push over the Kokoda Trail to capture Port Moresby was halted by the Australians in November.

the 21st and 25th Brigades assigned to Port Moresby, and the 18th Brigade posted to Milne Bay — and several American service and engineer units.

The Americans were on the move elsewhere with massed landings at Guadalcanal on August 7. They took the island's airfield the next day, but the Japanese retaliated with strong naval moves which put three American heavy cruisers and Australia's HMAS *Canberra* on the bottom of the Solomon Sea. Japan, however, could not follow up that success as most of its troops in the region were involved with the moves in and around New Guinea, but in a desperate attempt to force the Americans from the Solomons more than a battalion of soldiers was diverted to Guadalcanal, drawing them away from New Guinea at a critical point of the Japanese thrust towards Port Moresby.

While the fighting on Guadalcanal remained heavy and undecided, the Owen Stanleys were relatively quiet. The Japanese had not moved south from Isurava, and the Australians in New Guinea were settling-in a new commander, Lieutenant General Sydney Rowell. As well, the 39th Battalion, which had borne the brunt of Japan's aggression in New Guinea, had a new officer in charge, Lieutenant Colonel Ralph Honner. There was a new confidence amongst the Allies, the enemy seemingly slowed by their own lengthening supply and communication lines, as well as the trying terrain. Such difficulties, U.S. Intelligence assured Rowell, would prevent further enemy advances overland, but the Australian commander disagreed, believing steadfastly that the Japanese would attempt to move on Port Moresby by crossing the mountains.

Rowell now moved forward the 21st Brigade of the 7th Division commanded by Brigadier A.W. Potts. The war correspondent Osmar White asked Rowell about the wisdom of such a move, and the general's reply was blunt: "As far as I'm concerned, I'm willing to pull back and present the Jap with the supply problem I've got. But there are those who think otherwise. We need a victory in the Pacific and a lot of poor

8

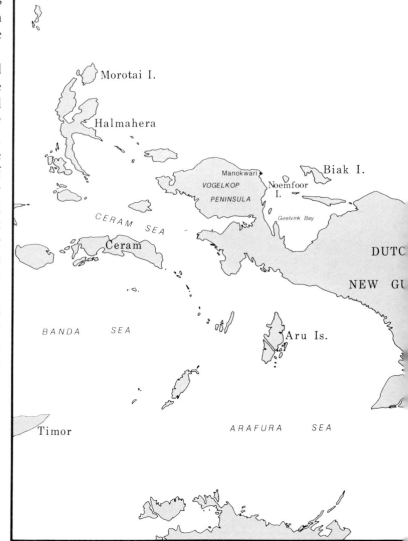

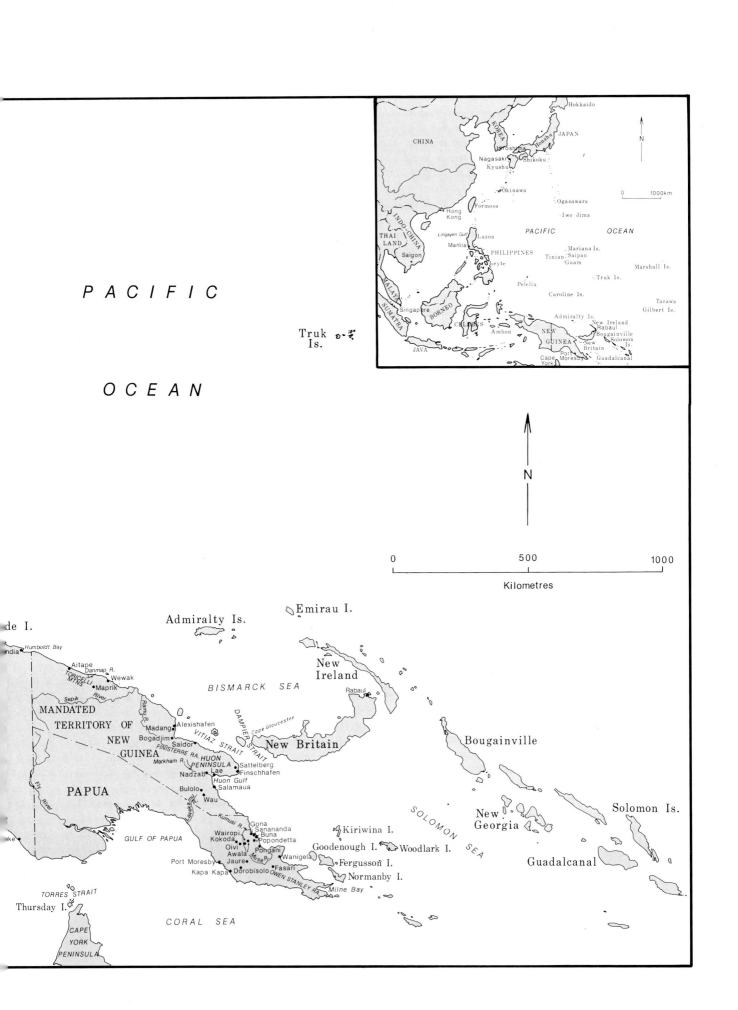

bastards have got to get killed to provide it."

Rowell also had other things on his mind, especially the fulfilment of his orders to prevent further penetration of Papua, to hold the crest of the Owen Stanley Range, and retake Kokoda, the Buna-Gona area and ultimately Lae and Salamaua. His administration problems were immense, especially those concerning supply, which had to be solved before any offensive operations could be carried out.

Despite such headaches, the Australian commander was confident. On August 21 he wrote to Blamey, "By this evening we will have four stripped battalions on the Range, 39, 53, 2/14, 2/16; about 2,000 men. We are all very well and in the highest of spirits."

Rowell, seemingly, had not heard that on the same day his brigade commander, Potts, discovered only five days' rations available at a dried-up lake bed called Myola, just south of Templeton's Crossing. It was one of the few places available for the air-dropping of supplies to the Australians, and although Rowell had been led to believe that 25 days' supplies were to be there, air-dropping techniques had yet to be perfected and 20 days' worth of goods had been lost in the jungle surrounding the lake bed. A worried Potts passed the information on to Rowell; the plans for his advance would have to be changed.

Two days later, Rowell wrote once more to Blamey: "This again raises the question of air support. Since August 17 only one plane has been available and that only for the past two days." Rowell had discovered that ration reserves forward of his position amounted to only 4,500 kilograms, but his force needed at least twice that each day merely for its maintenance. It was thought that around 20,000 kilos had been lost in the bush. And, although there were 30 transport aircraft in MacArthur's command, only half were available at any one time; many of these were used for ferrying generals. Extra transport aircraft were not available and MacArthur told Blamey that air-dropping should be used as an emergency, not as a normal means of supply. Rowell had to find

some other means of supplying his troops, and the crisis meant that until stocks had been built up he could not order major offensive operations by the newly arrived 7th Division.

Potts's force, however, was still deployed. The 2/14th Battalion and the 53rd Battalion were moved forward around Isurava and Alola on the main track to Kokoda. The 53rd, which so far had not been involved in any fighting, was given a pivotal role on the right flank, the 2/14th were to relieve the 39ers, which Potts described as "weak due to continuous work, lack of warm clothing, blankets, shelters, curtailed rations, being wet every night, a monotonous diet, combined with a comparatively static role for the last fortnight." The 2/16th Battalion was not brought forward because the Australians'

Advancing under shelter of a light tank, U.S. marines on Guadalcanal flush Japan 10,000 Americans seized the island's airfield, but after enemy reinforcemer

supply lines could simply not maintain a third battalion to the front in the ranges; the 2/16th Battalion was placed in reserve covering Myola.

The men of the 2/14th had seen hard fighting in Syria, and they were now anxious to get into action in New Guinea. Captain H.D. ''Blue'' Steward, the 2/16th's medical officer, watched the men of the 2/14th make their final preparations before moving forward. ''Nothing was left to chance,'' Steward said. ''Clothing and gear were doubly checked, boots studded to give their soles more grip, weapons cleaned; the men looked as keen as the bayonets they were grinding to razor-edge sharpness. As they glinted in the bright morning sun, I thought 'God help any Japanese on the receiving end.' ''

The sun also highlighted the men's uniforms, still the khaki shirts and shorts they had worn in North Africa and Syria, but now totally unsuited to New Guinea's verdant forests. Not only were jungle-green camouflage uniforms not yet available, General Blamey did not think that they were even necessary.

The men now humped their loads of more than 30 kilos from Port Moresby. Their motor transport carried them only a short distance, and then came the wearying march over terrain which one soldier in a report on the track commented was ''impossible for white men carrying loads.'' Yet, despite six days of terrible climbing, only one man from the battalion dropped out — and he had appendicitis.

At the end of that ordeal, they were to meet renewed advances by the Japanese. The 53rd

ldiers out of coastal jungle. In a massive amphibious assault on August 7, 1942, a force of
rived fierce battles for Guadalcanal raged until Allied conquest in February 1943.

Japanese troops teach village children "pidgin Japanese" songs as a form of indoctrination. Although promising liberation for the islanders, the Japanese Army treated Rabaul and Papuan carriers and labourers shockingly, driving them at bayonet point until they dropped, and denying them proper medical care.

Battalion, which had gone forward earlier, was stricken by equipment shortages and had already had several fierce contacts. One patrol went out to relieve another and collect its weapons at Missima village on a track verging eastward of the main Kokoda route at Alola. That secondary trail ran along a higher spur than that which carried the main track, and a strong enemy group on it could easily take an Australian force on a vulnerable flank.

The 53rd's platoon had gone out without weapons and left no one to delay an enemy advance southwards on that unexpected axis. The Australians saw Japanese moving in strength. When Potts heard of the affair he was appalled. It topped a series of disappointing episodes involving the 53rd, and he signalled the 7th Division's Major General A.S. Allen in Port Moresby, seeking the return to his brigade of the 2/27th Battalion: "The 53rd Battalion's training and discipline are below the standard required for action. Only use for holding objective aerodrome."

As an imminent Japanese attack built up, Potts again asked for the return of his third battalion, but Allen was not prepared to release them. He was responsible for the defence of Port Moresby, and the 2/27th could be needed there. Indeed, there was every possibility that that might be the case: on August 25 the Japanese began offensives in the Kokoda region, at Milne Bay, and from Lae and Salamaua towards Wau.

Early on the night of August 26, in the mountains south of Kokoda, Potts's force was in trouble. The Japanese attacked with five reinforced battalions, greatly outnumbering the Australians, who had no more than three battalions in the forward area. Using continuous flanking movements, the Japanese were able easily to move around the Australians and impede their withdrawal. One Japanese battalion's mission highlighted their intentions: "To advance along the eastern side of the valley, deploy to the south of Isurava, block the

Australians' withdrawal and annihilate them.''

The Australians were not prepared for such tactics of infiltration; even the battle-experienced men of the 2/14th Battalion, who had been used to fighting in the desert, were surprised. Osmar White wrote: ''They were more than half afraid of the country. You could see that in their movements, in their whole attitude. They were far more afraid of the country than the Japanese. They were continually worried by the idea of being 'cut off'. To their minds, being cut off meant that one must wander in the jungle, wander in the hills, wander in the valleys, up and down those heartbreaking razorbacks, until one died of hunger or exhaustion.''

Despite Potts's misgivings about the 53rd Battalion's abilities, he ordered them forward to Missima on August 27 in an attempt to stop the Japanese advance down the eastern spur. In the fierce fight that followed, the battalion's commanding officer, Lieutenant Colonel K.H. Ward, was killed and the two forward companies broke and ran. Potts's fears about their effectiveness were realised, and he pulled the 53rd out of the forward lines, giving them a task in the rear. Later, a captured Japanese account of this battle indicated that some of the 53rd Battalion soldiers had fought well, but another captured Japanese diary said simply, ''The Australians won't fight.'' No doubt the loss of their commanding officer contributed to the panic which gripped many of the young and inexperienced soldiers.

The other Australian militia battalion, the 39th, however showed its mettle. Its planned relief by the 2/14th was disrupted by the sudden Japanese attack, and around Isurava companies of both battalions now fought desperately from hastily prepared positions against the much

Veterans of the Middle East, two members of 2/14th Battalion share a crude jungle shelter on the Kokoda Trail. While one checks his submachine-gun before the next bloody engagement, his companion pens a letter home.

Former kangaroo-hunter, 2/5th Independent Company commando Private Harry Lake (left), and the youthful 39th Battalion militiaman, Corporal James Canty (right), show the tough and raw faces of New Guinea's tenacious defenders.

stronger Japanese. The attackers spent hours patiently studying the Australians' defensive layout, and then broke into the 39th's perimeter on the left flank where the tributary of the Eora Creek had cut a ravine some five metres deep and 20 metres wide.

When the assault was launched, one of the company commanders, Captain W.G.T. Merritt, was away from his position shaving in a nearby stream. His commanding officer, Lieutenant Colonel Ralph Honner, was washing as well and said coolly, ''Captain Merritt, will you go up to your company when you have finished your shave? The Japs have just broken through your perimeter.''

Merritt arrived at his company's position to discover that the Japanese had used the dead ground of the ravine cleverly, and once in it they were quickly reinforced. One observer wrote later, ''Through the widening breach poured another flood of attackers to swirl around the remainder of the right platoon from the rear. They were met with Bren gun and Tommy gun, with bayonet and grenade, but still they came,

to close with the buffet of fist and boot and rifle butt, the steel of crashing helmets and of strangling fingers.''

In the vicious man-to-man fighting that followed, Merritt's men faced annihilation, but two quick counter-attacks turned the battle around. One platoon drove out the enemy breaking through the gap and closed it against further inroads, and then a mobile reserve raced up to recapture the position. They were immediately successful, forcing the enemy back to the creek, and though the fighting continued throughout the afternoon the attackers made no further moves. That night the arriving companies of the 2/14th helped to restore the position and stabilise the defence.

Potts had been able to plug the hole for the time being, but soon the position again became desperate. His forward elements were under almost constant fire, and the Japanese were pressing everywhere, launching attack after attack against the 2/14th on the left and the 2/16th on the right, where they had taken over from the disgraced 53rd. The Japanese seemed fitter and better trained even than the elite troops of the AIF. And, certainly, they were better equipped, their heavier machine-guns causing terrible casualties among the Australians. Also, the enemy's physical appearance was surprising; many of the Australians were victims of propaganda that identified the Japanese as small, bandy-legged men with glasses and buckteeth. Many of them, however, were large men from the northern Japanese island of Hokkaido, and they were able to withstand the harsh climate of the Owen Stanleys much better than the Diggers.

Still, the best of the Australians in those rugged hills were equal to the toughest enemy. During the melee around Isurava, two platoons of the 39th Battalion were cut off, without food, but they finally made it back to the 2/14th's area and were quickly pressed back into service. The 2/16th's medical officer, Captain "Blue" Steward, saw the "boys" as he called them. They were, he wrote, "gaunt spectres with gaping boots and rotting tatters of uniform hanging around them like scarecrows. They were drained by malaria, dysentery and near starvation, but they were still in the firing line, facing a much more powerful enemy, equipped with much heavier weaponry."

Other members of the 2/16th were also impressed. One said, "When I saw those poor bastards, tottering on their bleeding, swollen feet, turn around and go straight back to Isurava, I knew they were good."

Such bravery was also seen amongst the wounded, for whom it was a living hell simply to get back to proper medical treatment. The medical officers tried hard, but they were short of supplies, of stretcher-bearers and areas to work on the wounded away from the Japanese mortar and artillery fire. Osmar White passed two soldiers on the track, one of whom had been shot through the left eye and the other through the foot. "The bullet," wrote White, "had passed obliquely and shallowly through his skull from just above the cheekbone, and emerged just behind the ear. He complained of severe headache, but said the wound itself was not painful. The man with the bullet through his foot was leading him. The pair had walked 113 miles (180 kilometres) in 16 days. They expected to reach the roadhead in another five." Such journeys were faced by every wounded man. There were simply no other methods of evacuating the casualties.

Although the Australians had managed to hold the Japanese forces during the first few days of this renewed onslaught, making only small withdrawals and, in many cases, being able to restore lost positions, from August 29 the situation began to deteriorate badly. On that day, the Japanese launched a series of powerful attacks against the forward Australian battalion positions, with Major General Tomitaro Horii having more than six infantry battalions at his disposal. Potts had less than half that number. As well, the Japanese had the advantage of high ground, dominating the Australian positions on both sides of a narrow valley.

On the right, the 2/16th Battalion was first bumped by a force of about 100 Japanese supported by two heavy machine-guns which they had dug in for the attack. This thrust was repulsed, but the Australians did not have sufficient forces to mount an effective counter.

On the left, the Japanese pushed hard against the 2/14th Battalion's position. Here, bitter hand-to-hand fighting right through the morning forced the Australians back, and by early afternoon the Japanese had penetrated so far into the battalion's position that the 2/14th's headquarters was threatened. A composite group of soldiers from several companies now came together and counter-attacked. Private Bruce Kingsbury, whose platoon had already been badly mauled that day, joined the action, picking up a Bren gun and racing forward, shooting from the hip. Japanese machine-gunners fired back desperately, but somehow missed as the young Victorian continued to clear a path of more than 100 metres through the assaulting Japanese. But just as he had halted the enemy attack, a single shot rang out from the jungle; Kingsbury was killed. For his extraordinary actions that day, he was awarded

THE KOKODA TRAIL

Foot-slogging through thick mud on the Kokoda Trail, Diggers pass an abandoned bicycle. In the rugged highlands, soldiers sweated in humid heat, shivered in frost and hail, and were drenched in sudden violent downpours of rain.

The Kokoda Trail earned a reputation as one of the Pacific war's greatest tests of strength and endurance. Few intrepid Europeans had used the track before the war, as it was considered passable to only the region's barefooted natives. But with the Owen Stanley Range vital in the hostilities, thousands of heavily booted soldiers tramped the Kokoda Trail into a deep quagmire. This morass was kept saturated by an annual rainfall of 250 centimetres.

The track made no attempt to follow an easy gradient. Its altitude "altered like a switch back railway," said Brigadier S.H.W.C. Porter, 30th Brigade. From Port Moresby, a road climbed 40 kilometres to the edge of a plateau in the Owen Stanley foothills. Here all motor transport ended and a foot trail began near the village of Ilolo. From there the trail fell gently for a few kilometres until it reached Ower's Corner and then suddenly dropped sharply through dense forests and across swift streams to Uberi village. From Uberi along the banks of the Goldie River the going was reasonably easy until a climb up a steep razor-edged spur to Imita Ridge tested the toughest of leg muscles. Engineers had cut more than 2,000 timber steps into the muddy slope, and they were ironically dubbed the "Golden Stairs".

From Imita Ridge the vista of the Owen Stanleys' mist-enshrouded peaks filled the pack-laden Digger with weary apprehension. The track now plunged down another knife-edge spur into a stream about 400 metres below, following its course for about five kilometres. Then came a dizzying 600-metre climb to Iori-baiwa Ridge, followed by another tor-turous 300-metre descent before a strenuous 750-metre hike to the crest of the Maguli Range. The engineers had cut 3,500 steps into this slope. The next village on the trail was Nauro, on the banks of the Brown River, which the track followed through thick scrub until another gut-wrenching ascent up and over a mountain arrived at Menari village.

The real climb was still to come. An arduous trek uphill continued over broken ridges until it suddenly dropped into an open valley to arrive at Efogi village. The track rose steeply for almost 550 metres to Kagi village and then climbed another 800 metres through dense, dank rainforest to "the Gap". Interpreted from maps by commanders away from the front, the Gap was imagined as some sort of alpine pass that could be easily held by a resolute band of men. But, in fact, it was simply an 11-kilometre-wide break in the mountains through which aircraft could fly at low altitudes. The trail crested here to begin its quick descent to the narrow valley of Eora Creek where it snaked its way around slippery spurs high above the creek on one side of the valley. Suddenly it fell to ford the raging torrent of Eora Creek at Templeton's Crossing. Climbing high up the other side of the valley it took another steep plunge to Eora Creek village on a flat platform overhanging the turbulent creek below. The trail kept rising to Alola and took a slippery, precipitous route to the next village, Isurava. From there to Deniki was marginally less difficult, and at Deniki the soldier looked across the fertile Yodda valley to see Kokoda village and its strategic airstrip. From Kokoda the trip to the wire-rope bridge (*Wairopi* in Pidgin) across the Kumusi River was an easy trail through scrub-covered foothills.

Little wonder that the Diggers' experiences on this heart-wrenching and back-breaking trail became part of Australia's military legends.

Soldiers and native carriers negotiate the 3,500 steps cut by Australian engineers for the steep ascent to Nauro village.

En route to Templeton's Crossing, heavily burdened 16th Brigade soldiers reach the crest of Mount Bellamy Ridge.

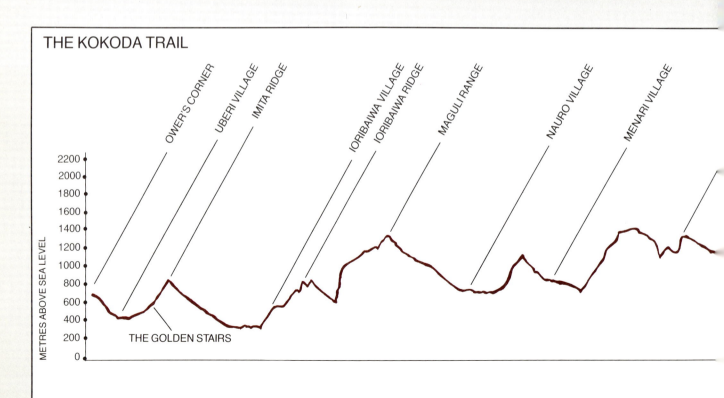

THE KOKODA TRAIL

OWER'S CORNER

UBERI VILLAGE

IMITA RIDGE

IORIBAIWA VILLAGE

IORIBAIWA RIDGE

MAGULI RANGE

NAURO VILLAGE

MENARI VILLAGE

METRES ABOVE SEA LEVEL

2200
2000
1800
1600
1400
1200
1000
800
600
400
200
0

THE GOLDEN STAIRS

On their way to Wairopi, troops trudge in single file over a rickety footbridge crossing one of the many creeks running through the deep valleys of the Owen Stanley Range.

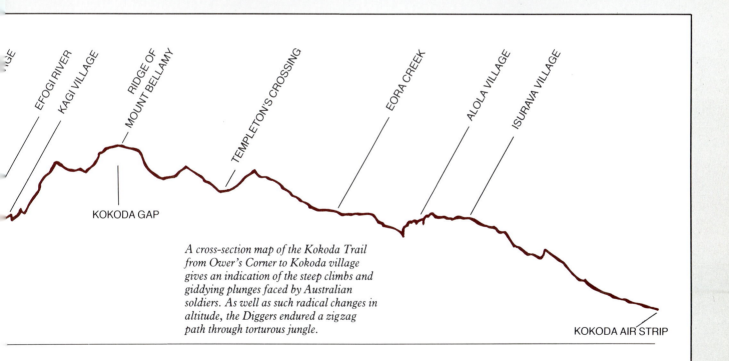

EFOGI RIVER

KAGI VILLAGE

RIDGE OF
MOUNT BELLAMY

TEMPLETON'S CROSSING

EORA CREEK

ALOLA VILLAGE

ISURAVA VILLAGE

KOKODA GAP

A cross-section map of the Kokoda Trail from Ower's Corner to Kokoda village gives an indication of the steep climbs and giddying plunges faced by Australian soldiers. As well as such radical changes in altitude, the Diggers endured a zigzag path through torturous jungle.

KOKODA AIR STRIP

An eloquent scene is captured on film by AIF cameraman Damien Parer during the 21st Brigade's retreat from Kokoda: a wounded infantryman receives a light from a Salvation Army officer on the track.

a posthumous Victoria Cross.

Despite such bravery, the situation was irretrievable for the Australians. On the night of August 29, General Horii issued an order which not only predicted the imminent annihilation of the Australian forces, but also indicated how good Japanese Intelligence really was: "There are still some remnants in a section of the position, and their spirit is extremely high. The Australian 39th Battalion has been reinforced, and taking advantage of the rugged terrain, they appear to put up a serious resistance."

Horii ordered his troops to capture the Australian positions confronting them, and to prepare for further action. That they did, pushing well inside each of the forward battalion posts. Potts had no option but to order a withdrawal to Alola the following morning.

The following day, Potts's brigade was continually forced back, and this time it was the 2/14th who suffered most grievously, losing 170 men. Remnants of the battalion were cut off

during the fighting withdrawal, including the 2/14th's commander, Lieutenant A.S. Key, and his battalion headquarters group. After splitting into several parties, they tried to get along the Eora Creek back to the Australian positions, but the going was tough and the Japanese were everywhere. Key's group was later ambushed again, but four of his men broke away and struggled on. After many days of hunger and torturous slogging, two men died, and six weeks after that scrambling escape from the Japanese near Alola, the other two stumbled into a welcome group of Australian engineers.

Key and five others, however, had stayed in the jungle and were captured. The lieutenant was then transported via a Buna gaol to Rabaul, but he was never heard of again.

Other groups of soldiers cut off from the main Alola withdrawal also endured a hellish time returning to safety. Captain S.H. Buckler and some of his company went along the line of Eora Creek, unable to get back onto the track above

Cut off from the main withdrawal over the Kokoda Trail, stragglers of 2/14th Battalion arrive after six desperate weeks, weak with hunger and exhaustion, at an American base in October 1942. Their rafts were built by friendly natives.

them because the Japanese were on it. Buckler and his men carried two soldiers on stretchers, three others were wounded but walking, and Corporal J.A. Metson, shot in the ankle, refused to be carried either on another man's back or a stretcher. "It will take eight of you chaps to carry that thing," Metson told them. "Throw it away. I'll get along somehow." The young corporal bandaged his hands and knees, and crawled the rest of the way.

They soon came upon another group of 2/14th men who had been carrying a 39th Battalion sergeant on a stretcher throughout the night. As well, off in the jungle away from his mates, they found Private A. Mayne, who had been supported on the back of a fit soldier. Now he had stolen away into the woods to hide, no longer wishing to burden his fellows.

Buckler eventually sent one group back towards Myola to find help, and after running into a Japanese patrol, of which the Australians were able to kill three, the Diggers made it back,

via Dorobisolo, to their battalion in early October. Buckler, however, backtracked towards Sengai, between Kokoda and Wairopi, that route being easier and planted with native food. Metson continued to crawl, virtually starving and racked by cold and pain. Friendly locals showed them the way, and after 10 days they reached Sengai where eight men, including Metson and Mayne, were left. Buckler and 38 others then headed off via the Kumusi River, going upstream towards Jaure, then to Dorobisolo before reaching an American camp to the south. Just one soldier died of his wounds on the way, but those who remained at Sengai were killed later by the Japanese.

Theirs had been an extraordinary flight from the fearsome battle at Alola. One officer who took part in the general withdrawal said that the journey had tortured the walking wounded and the stretcher cases. "All night long, a stumbling procession moved up the track. It was bad enough in daylight. On such a night, in

Men of the 2/33rd Battalion march with heavy packs and stout walking sticks across the Brown River. They were fresh reinforcements for the Australians' fightback to Kokoda.

torrential rain which beat down unceasingly, along the greasy ditch deep in soupy mud went the columns of wounded men. They moved at a crawling pace, groping for each foothold, the strongest at the head of the column, the weakest at its end, each clutching the man ahead for support and guidance in the black darkness.''

Osmar White reported that one party came in with a story of having trekked for kilometres just under the crest of a steep ridge, parallel with a party of Japanese. ''No one on either side was willing to show his head against the skyline for a shot,'' White wrote, ''so they fought it out by tossing grenades at one another, over the crest. The Mills grenade won.'' He said the battle remained without form. The Australians had no fresh troops and every man who took part in the battle for the Owen Stanleys was exhausted. They had been fed in piecemeal and defeated in detail. The enemy was in complete command of the situation.

On September 1, the Japanese attacked the 2/16th's position at Alola, and Potts was forced to pull back even further. His men were in tatters, but now reinforcements were on the way, with two fresh 25th Brigade battalions, the 2/31st and 2/33rd, the militia 3rd Battalion, the 2/1st Pioneers, and the 2/6th Independent Company which was to patrol to the west of the main track.

Potts himself was considered by his generals to be too stressed to continue, and Brigadier S.H.W.C. Porter took over the forward Australian positions on September 10. Now he faced pulling back his tired troops, and of two ridges to his south, Ioribaiwa and Imita, he preferred Imita, on which he figured he could regather his men to stage an effective counter-attack. However, he received ill-advised orders to hold yet another ridge to the north of Ioribaiwa. As the terrain there was totally unsuitable, Porter retired to Ioribaiwa itself, where he and his soldiers withstood heavy Japanese shelling and constant attacking probes. By September 14, the new battalions, commanded by Brigadier K.W. Eather, were in position, but General Horii also began another concerted thrust at Port Moresby. Heavy fighting ensued for two days, by which time Eather now realised that Imita Ridge was in fact the best place for defence. He withdrew the troops superbly, and by September 20 they were well-entrenched.

From here, there could be no turning back. Rowell, ever practical and aware of his enemy's difficulties, issued orders to the 7th Division: "Stress the fact that however many troops the enemy has, they must have walked all the way from Buna. We are now so far back that any further withdrawal is out of the question. Eather must fight it out at all costs."

Rowell was buying time; he knew that the Japanese would face exactly the same supply problems his own troops had encountered. And he was waiting for the 25th Brigade to establish control between Ioribaiwa and Imita. Eather, luckily, had some time and the opportunity to organise his forces.

Potts, who was eventually relieved of his command, had never been able to organise his brigade properly on its arrival, but instead committed it company by company while withdrawing against a stronger enemy. He had also faced a supply system which failed to sufficiently provide for his forces. And he had been unable to make a clean break away from the Japanese to withdraw to an easily defended position. Eather now had Imita Ridge, the first good defensive position the Australians had occupied since pulling back from Kokoda.

Potts carried the blame for a failure that was not his fault. Later, Rowell wrote that the brigade's "devotion and courage in the face of great odds, both from the enemy and the environment, delayed the Japanese until a force could be assembled for the counter-stroke."

Rowell certainly appreciated the problems faced by Potts and his men, much more than either Blamey or MacArthur, but Rowell was unable to help Potts. So much depended upon the availability of supplies and transport, which had been severely restricted.

And Rowell's tasks were not helped by the panic in MacArthur's headquarters. America's official historian remarked, "All this time General Headquarters had been under the impression that the Japanese strength on the trail was slight, and that the enemy had no real intention of advancing on Port Moresby." Allied Intelligence, at least down at operational level, was very sketchy; the knowledge of the terrain over which these men were fighting was even more limited. At one stage, MacArthur's headquarters had ordered that the Owen Stanley Range was to be prepared for demolition. Rowell replied, asking wryly whether it was "this week's funny story".

The campaign revealed the enormous gap between the experiences of the front-line soldiers and the understanding of their commanders. Later, at a special parade of the 21st Brigade, Blamey spoke to the men of the two battered AIF battalions, the 2/14th and the 2/16th. He told them they had been beaten by inferior troops in inferior numbers. "It is," said the tactless general, "the rabbit that runs away that gets shot." The parade nearly erupted. Two weeks after that sorry occasion, Blamey inspected some wounded 21st Brigade soldiers in hospital at Port Moresby. They were all sitting up in bed nibbling on lettuce leaves!

Back in Brisbane, during the first week of September 1942, while the Australians were pulling back and suffering the worst of the Japanese thrust to Port Moresby, MacArthur was busily trying to plan an amphibious operation against the northern coast of Papua. There were no spare ships, so MacArthur tried another approach: the sending of large numbers of ground reinforcements to Papua while making creeping advances along the coast. Such a course, MacArthur told U.S. Army Chief of Staff General George Marshall, would "secure a situation which otherwise is doubtful. If New Guinea goes the result will be disastrous."

MacArthur readily blamed the Australian soldiers in his appraisal of the campaign, claiming that they were "unable to match the enemy in jungle fighting." But the mud did not stick. Although one battalion had performed badly in the mountains, the others had kept a

SUPPLY CRISIS

Using walking sticks for balance, two barefoot native porters shoulder cargo on a slippery, trackless slope of the Kokoda Trail. Although Australian soldiers were heavily burdened with equipment, natives became indispensable for supply.

The war in New Guinea became a war of supply. Throughout the long and bloody Kokoda Trail campaign, both the Australians and Japanese were beset with acute supply problems, and the movement of their forces was dictated by the availability of materiel. Every round of ammunition, every mortar bomb and every tin of food had to be carried over a thickly jungled mountain track that was impassable to motor transport and pack animals.

Even before Japan's invasion of New Guinea a former planter, Lieutenant Bert Kienzle, was given the task of organising a native carrier force and establishing a series of staging posts, a day's march apart, along the Kokoda Trail. Kienzle commandeered horses and mules to run a pack relay, and he had native carrier-trains as far forward as Isurava. The key to maintaining supply levels in such harsh country, however, was

air-dropping, and he discovered a clearing named Myola suitable for such delivery. But Myola was still three days' haul from the front line, and native carriers continued to play their vital role. Even so, all staging posts along the track remained inadequately supplied, and Australian front-line troops were withdrawn.

The Japanese pushed ahead, gambling on capturing Australian stores and quickly seizing Port Moresby. To speed their advance, they skimped on their own supplies except ammunition, but the Australians destroyed all their dumps as they withdrew. Soon the Japanese found that their supply line stretched all the way from Buna on the northeastern coast to Ioribaiwa Ridge. Over-extended and under constant Allied air attack, the Japanese weakened every day.

The Australians retaliated, and by bringing their supply crisis under control, holding strategic dumping

grounds along the trail, improving bureaucratic checks on quantities, and winning back the airfield at Kokoda, the Allies seized the initiative. Their air-transport program became more efficient as pilots and crews perfected their techniques. Accurate location of dropping areas was helped by using burnt patches and log-patterns on the ground as markers. And an optimum height and speed of delivery was calculated to avoid smashing or losing packages. Then, with cargo stacked in the open doorways of Douglas aircraft, the planes made successive runs over a dropping area; "pusherouters", strapped-in with safety belts now thrust the cargo out with their feet.

Such skills and the continual courage of Allied transport aircrews in the hostile skies over New Guinea kept the Diggers on the ground fed and equipped for their bloody clash with the Japanese.

The "Pony Express", with a 72-kilo pack per animal, climbs the narrow, winding track to Uberi in single file. There, supply-bags were distributed to native porters.

After a signal from the pilot, an army air-maintenance crew launch a stack of vital goods from the open doorway of a Douglas aircraft. Most supplies, both free-dropped and parachute-dropped, were "kicked off" in this way.

During their efforts to extend the Allied supply line to Buna in November 1942, Australian engineers construct a bridge for heavy supply traffic next to a wire-suspension footbridge across the swirling rapids of the Kumusi River.

superior force out of Port Moresby.

And, at Milne Bay where the Japanese had launched an offensive on August 25 to coincide with its Kokoda push, the enemy met staunch opposition. The Japanese had planned to take the strategically important bay on Papua's extreme east coast as part of their coordinated drive towards Port Moresby. Not only could the bay provide excellent shelter for shipping, but near its western edge were three well-engineered airstrips. However, an Allied force had occupied the area. The Australians consisted of the militia 7th Brigade group, two squadrons of RAAF Kittyhawks, No. 75 and No. 76, and the AIF 18th Brigade. And as well as two anti-aircraft batteries, one battery of an artillery field regiment, and one of anti-tank guns, there were two American engineer units and two batteries of U.S. anti-aircraft guns. In charge of the total force was Major General Cyril Clowes.

The Japanese landed a massive force in and around the bay on August 25/26, but concerted defence by the Australian infantry and the RAAF's total control of the air soon turned back the enemy. The attackers virtually spent themselves in the first few days of the battle, fighting the dogged Australians as well as the impossibly swampy terrain. By the first week in September the Japanese were well beaten.

It was Nippon's first defeat of the war on land, and it negated one of Japan's major thrusts at Port Moresby. The enemy threat, however, was still strong, and on September 13/14 Japan struck once again at American forces on Guadalcanal. But the attack was turned back. Now, combined with the defeat at Milne Bay, Japan's Imperial General Headquarters was in trouble, and ordered that all possible forces be directed towards the Solomons; the battle there would continue to seesaw throughout September and October.

Such a turnaround, especially the success at Milne Bay, was lost on Australia's politicians, who were more concerned about the rapid withdrawals over the Kokoda Trail. The Australian Commander-in-Chief, General Blamey, was asked to go to New Guinea to assess the situation for himself, and after a short trip he returned confident that the Australians would push back the Japanese. After speaking with Rowell and Allen in New Guinea, he assured Australia's Advisory War Council that Port Moresby would not fall.

While admitting that the situation on the Kokoda Trail was far from satisfactory, he did not tell the council the whole truth — that in fact the Australians of Eather's 25th Brigade had been forced to withdraw south of Ioribaiwa to Imita Ridge. Perhaps Blamey feared that the politicians would not understand the reasons for such a move, or that the initiative was beginning to pass to the Australians, particularly with the imminent arrival in Port Moresby of the 16th Brigade.

In fact, the withdrawal made sound tactical sense, because it gave the hard-pressed Australian forces an opportunity to regroup and prepare to push the Japanese back across the Owen Stanley Range. By aggressive patrolling between September 17 and September 24, Eather's men were able to establish a clear superiority over the Japanese between Imita and Ioribaiwa, providing the basis for a subsequent offensive. At this stage as well, the Australians had artillery support for the first time in the New Guinea campaign: some 25-pounders of the 14th Field Regiment were brought into play as Eather dominated no-man's-land in front of the Japanese forces, readying his men for a major counter-attack. Now, too, the Australians of the 25th Brigade shed another of their disadvantages — their khaki uniforms. During September they were the first Diggers to wear jungle green.

That period also saw a crisis develop over Blamey's dual role as MacArthur's deputy and his position as Commander-in-Chief, Australian Military Forces. MacArthur wanted Blamey to go to New Guinea, but the Australian general already had a senior soldier there, Sydney Rowell, who was considered by Blamey to be more than capable. With his own position in jeopardy, however, Blamey arrived there on September 23, and Rowell's command became

Members of the 14th Field Regiment, helped by 2/1st Pioneer Battalion, haul a 25-pounder field gun up a slippery track near Uberi village. The battery's urgently needed guns opened fire on enemy positions on September 20.

untenable. He was sacked on the first day of the Australian advance back towards Kokoda.

While the Australian commanders were sorting out their senior positions, the Japanese were also having a change of heart. Although General Horii's forces had come close to Port Moresby, and their patrols could see the ocean from Ioribaiwa, they had failed to capture their main objective. Now with their defeat at Milne Bay and increasing difficulties in Guadalcanal, this objective was postponed. Horii's forces were also running out of food, and even as the last Australians left Ioribaiwa Ridge, the Japanese were more interested in any rations that might have remained behind rather than in following up the withdrawal.

On September 20, shortly after telling his subordinate commanders that they were pausing only to regain their strength before the final push on Port Moresby, Horii received orders to withdraw from Ioribaiwa to a defensive perimeter around Buna and Gona. He left behind his 14th Regiment at the Eora Creek-Templeton's Crossing area with orders to hold any advance of the Australians.

The decision to withdraw was greeted bitterly by many Japanese soldiers. One wrote in his diary: "It is a sorry thing that we must leave the bodies of our comrades and the ground we have won so dearly. Sleep peacefully my friends. Farewell: We shall meet again in Heaven." As the Japanese fighting soldiers withdrew back across the trail, their service troops around Buna worked feverishly building bunkers, digging gun positions, cutting fire-lanes and preparing the entire position for a bitter and protracted defence.

The Australian offensive on Ioribaiwa Ridge began on September 28, and when the attack went in the Australian troops encountered no opposition. The Japanese had slipped away at the last moment, abandoning strongly prepared positions along with large quantities of equipment. "Many Japanese bodies have been found in an emaciated condition showing all evidence of starvation and dysentery," wrote George Johnston. "Many of the Japs have been eating grass, wood, weeds, roots and poisonous fruits. The air in the misty valleys is heavy with the stench of death."

The 16th Brigade diarist wrote: "Along the route were skeletons picked clean by rats and other vermin, and in the dark recesses came to our nostrils the stench of the dead, some hastily buried or perhaps not buried at all."

As the Australians pushed forward across the trail, they also discovered that the Japanese had left behind them a trail of destruction of native villages and gardens. There was also evidence of atrocities against the unfortunate natives and Australian soldiers caught during the hectic withdrawal. Members of the 3rd Battalion came across the bodies of two Australian stragglers: one had been decapitated, the other bayoneted while his wrists were tied to a tree with wire.

Slowly and purposefully the Australians pushed back across the trail. The going was no easier than before, and again the old problems of supplying troops across such inhospitable terrain made commanders' tasks extremely difficult. Warrant Officer Bill Crooks, of the 2/33rd Battalion, recalled that "the speed of our advance was now solely controlled by our

Soldiers of the 16th Brigade, recently returned from the Middle East, begin their advance from Ower's Corner in October 1942. At Efogi village they encountered the skeletons and stench of unburied Australian dead, killed weeks before.

ability to get rations. In this strange and arduous campaign, operations were to be dictated by the administrative ability to maintain rations and ammunition forward. There would never be enough native carriers to allow a brigade to advance as we had been trained.''

The soldiers and officers on the trail, hungry and half-starved most of the time, knew this truth much more clearly than their commanders in Port Moresby and in Brisbane. The Australian advance was deliberately slow, however, as they pushed along side tracks methodically clearing every metre of the jungle as they went. They wanted to be certain that there would be no chance of ambush or raids from Japanese units still in the mountains.

MacArthur had now developed his plan for the next stage of the Papuan campaign. Unsure of the outcome of the vicious and unceasing battle for the Solomons, he aimed his offensive at enveloping and destroying the Japanese at their Buna beachhead. Expecting the enemy to hold tightly on to the best positions on the Kokoda Trail, MacArthur sought to outflank the mountains, advancing available troops on three axes: along the track via Kokoda and Wairopi; over the Kapa Kapa-Jaure track to the east; and up the coast northwestward from Milne Bay.

Now, too, with the danger to Port Moresby gone, MacArthur made his way to the front, arriving in New Guinea on October 2, 1942. He spent just two days there, mainly inspecting the Port Moresby area with Blamey, the Australian Army Minister Frank Forde, and the Melbourne barrister and artillery officer Lieutenant General Edmund Herring, who had taken over from the sacked Rowell. The American general also went to the beginning of the Kokoda Trail where he met Brigadier John ''Killer'' Lloyd, whose 16th Brigade was just about to begin its advance. The 16th Brigade had been one of the first raised in 1939 and, despite having suffered heavily in Greece and Crete, was one of the most experienced and best brigades in the AIF.

In a typically theatrical fashion, MacArthur said to the bemused Australian brigadier: 31

"Lloyd, by some act of God, your brigade has been chosen for this job. The eyes of the Western world are upon you and your men. Good luck and don't stop." Corporal Kenny Clift, a signaller with 16th Brigade headquarters, later recalled, "He then vaulted into our jeep and roared off, leaving our brigadier bewildered and stunned."

MacArthur might have told Lloyd not to stop, but it was not until supply problems were partially overcome that the Australian brigade was in a position to do so. Certainly ahead of Lloyd, Eather's 25th Brigade ran into immense difficulties with air supplies from the "biscuit bombers". There were always too few aircraft to go around, and communications between the forward and rear areas were always bad. Staff officers in Brisbane and in Port Moresby seemed to assume that all the rations and resupplies sent were automatically received,

but in reality only 10 per cent of some airdrops were recovered.

Accidents were also rife, and heavy casualties often occurred when mortar bombs exploded on impact with the ground after being dropped from air transports, or later when dropped into the tubes ready for firing. One entire mortar crew who had been right through the Middle East and Greece together was lost when a mortar bomb exploded. "The barrel of the mortar split like a banana in a dozen pieces," Kenny Clift recalled. "Meggsy (Sergeant Meggsy Madigan of the 2/1st Battalion) deafened, both ear drums blown, shrapnel wounds right around forehead and temples, blood streaming from ears, eyes, mouth and nose, was carried away on a stretcher, weeping bitterly, not for himself but for that tight little group of mates, his pride and joy."

Such incidents were depressingly common, almost as much as the hunger and exhaustion, the dampness and the cold endured by the troops on the Kokoda Trail. As well, supply difficulties were to have severe consequences among the higher levels of command in the Australian Army.

As part of MacArthur's plans to retake the Buna-Gona area, Major General A.S. Allen, commanding the 7th Division, had been ordered by Blamey to capture Kokoda and its airstrip. Once it was back in Australian hands, supply difficulties would be relieved and the momentum of the Australian advance raised. In Port Moresby, however, Blamey was now applying pressure to the Australian divisional commander. A bitter exchange of signals took place in which Allen reminded Blamey that the rate of advance was being retarded because of the shortage of supplies. Blamey's reply was abrupt: "In view lack of serious opposition your advance appears much too slow." Allen tried hard to make Blamey understand that the speed of the advance did not depend entirely on airdrops. "This country," he signalled, "is much tougher than any previous theatre and cannot be appreciated until seen."

Meanwhile, Brigadier Eather's brigade was

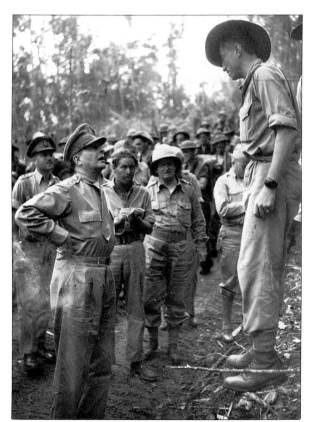

During his two-day Kokoda Trail inspection tour as far as Ower's Corner, General Douglas MacArthur talks with an Australian officer while an aide records his comments.

Supplies for the 25th and 16th Brigades are carried by pack-horse on a steep winding track while a field gun waits to be pulled, with ropes strapped to tree-stump posts, into the Uberi Valley and then up Imita Ridge.

preparing for an attack against the Japanese rearguard at Templeton's Crossing, where enemy troops of the 2nd Battalion, 144th Infantry Regiment, were entrenched on high ground on both sides of the Eora Creek gorge. Their positions were well sited, with dug-in machine-gun positions capable of supporting each other, with cleared fire-lanes and with well-protected flanks.

For two days the Australians of the 2/25th and 2/33rd battalions probed the thick bush and bamboo forward of Templeton's Crossing where the Japanese had established themselves. But they could make little progress. Then, as the 3rd Battalion came into the action, moving forward on October 15, they discovered the Japanese positions abandoned. The enemy, following their orders, had delayed the attackers for a few extra days, and then they had fallen back to the next defence line. The Australians pressed on, coming up against occasional ambush parties and small enemy groups set in the jungle to further harass them. After five days, Eather's men were still clawing their way to the top of the ridges, taking machine-gun positions and each weapon pit one by one.

On October 17, one company of the 3rd Battalion, Captain W.J.S. Atkinson's, came upon a typical enemy position, a party of Japanese firmly dug in, their machine-gun blocking the way. But Captain B.G.D. Tongs crawled up a fire-lane, dodging the enemy's shots before tossing a grenade right into their midst. "The two Japs in the pit were blown clean out," recalled Atkinson, "and sprawled one on each other — dead. That started the ball rolling. The men got excited and began yelling and whooping."

The Australians raced forward, but they met strong opposition. One platoon commander, Lieutenant C.H. Richardson, was hit in the chest, and he collapsed behind a tree, breathing desperately through the hole a bullet had made. Atkinson went in to help him, and the sniper responsible for the injured man took another shot, this time at the captain. The bullet went between his pack and back, hitting his dixie. The enemy sniper's muzzle blast was spotted by Private D. Downes, who with his pipe in his mouth, moved into the open to get a better aim, and shot him. Downes then retired quietly behind a tree, took his pipe from his mouth, and remarked coolly to his mates, "Well, I got that bastard."

The men of the 3rd Battalion continued to press home their attacks against staunch defence and sporadic counter-attacks. Despite mounting casualties — two forward companies lost seven men killed and 11 wounded — the Australians were making some headway. Then, on that same day, the hard-pressed Major General Allen received another angry signal from Blamey: "General MacArthur considers quote extremely light casualties indicate no serious effort yet made to displace enemy unquote. You will attack enemy with energy and all possible speed at each point of resistance." MacArthur was applying pressure on Blamey, who in turn was applying it to Allen. Neither MacArthur nor Blamey had been forward of Port Moresby to see for themselves the Australians' battle conditions. The senior command thought that wide encircling movements through the jungle were possible; both Blamey and MacArthur complained that the advance so far had been conducted on too narrow a front. But the reality was that the terrain did not allow for great sweeping movements behind the Japanese positions, nor was it easy to keep great numbers of troops in direct contact with the enemy. And, even if the fighting troops were not confined to the tracks, the resupplies certainly were.

Allen's troops had suffered heavily enough in this phase. The 25th Brigade had lost 68 killed, 135 wounded and 771 evacuated with illness. Now the 16th Brigade had caught up with the 25th Brigade battalions at Templeton's Crossing, and with the boom of mortar fire and the rattle of small arms echoing in the distance, Kenny Clift saw what the jungle fighting had wrought. He wrote: "We had been out of Moresby for about 14 days and although we

A patrol of 2/33rd Battalion probes along the banks of the Brown River through tall, razor-sharp kunai grass. Small fierce actions with retreating enemy troops climaxed in the 25th Brigade's prolonged battle at Templeton's Crossing.

looked fairly dilapidated, we were 'dandies' alongside the poor emaciated bastards who were once fit Australian troops of the 2/31st and 2/33rd battalions.''

The Japanese were also suffering at the Eora Creek gorge, for it was there that grim evidence of Japan's own supply plight was discovered. The bodies of two Australian soldiers, killed some days earlier, were discovered to have large portions of the arms, calves and thighs cut off. As well, a medical officer examined a parcel of meat discovered in a Japanese position by one of the patrols: ''One was the muscle tissue of a

large animal,'' he reported, ''the other similar muscle tissue with a large piece of skin and underlying tissues attached. I consider the last as human.''

By October 20, the 16th Brigade had replaced the 25th at the front, and was now ready to go into battle. The next day, when the attack went in, revealed that the Japanese had retired once again, this time to what one senior officer called the ''most formidable position on the whole length of the trail from Port Moresby to Kokoda.'' At the northern end of the Eora Creek gorge the Japanese rearguard held a strong defensive position, from which they could fire down on the Australian attackers from all directions. Lloyd told his battalion commanders that it was no good sustaining heavy losses in a frontal attack and then letting the Japanese retire to another prepared position. "What has to be our aim from now on is that each rearguard, left by the enemy to oppose us, has to be completely destroyed," Lloyd said. "By God that's the way we are going to fight. They won't settle back into the jungle to have another bite of the cherry. Is that understood?"

As the orders group received their plan, bullets slapped into the trees above them. The Japanese remaining in the mountains were not to be taken lightly, and the Australians still had the job ahead of them. It was clear that the Japanese position at Eora Creek was well-prepared and would take probably a brigade attack to move. The terrain here favoured the defenders; the Diggers were forced to attack across two small bridges over the fast-flowing creek, both directly observed by the enemy. The 16th Brigade battalions were below strength, with companies away on tasks on the flanks. But the pressure to push on was great.

On October 21, Blamey again signalled Allen: "During the last five days you have made practically no advance against a weaker enemy. Bulk of your forces have been defensively located in rear although enemy has shown no capacity to advance." And then, on the same day, Blamey passed on a signal he had received from MacArthur. Allen was told: "Operations report show our progress on the trail is not repeat not satisfactory. The tactical handling of our troops in my opinion is faulty. Our supply situation and the condition of our troops certainly compares favourably with those of the enemy and weather conditions are neutral." Allen drafted a reply to MacArthur's latest demands: "If you think you can do any better come up here and bloody well try." He was, however, persuaded by a calmer staff officer that to send such an impertinent reply might invite retribution.

Lloyd's brigade began its next attack on October 23. Over four days and nights the experienced AIF soldiers inched their way upwards against the Japanese, who had the advantage of the high ground. The Japanese mortar crews only had to land their bombs in the trees above the Australians and the resulting shower of shrapnel did the rest. The Australians were "clinging like limpets to what were almost intolerable positions, under constant fire and strain," said Kenny Clift. They suffered, too, from the cold and the rain. There was no way of getting hot food to them, and even smoke from a wispy, wet-wood fire to make a brew of tea would bring an immediate shower of grenades and machine-gun bursts from the enemy, who were literally only metres away.

Despite the deplorable conditions the morale of the 2/1st Battalion's men was still high. But their bodies could no longer respond to the demands being placed on them. The rain, by now torrential, had swelled the waters of the Eora Creek and made the task of evacuating the wounded even more of a nightmare. The battalion commanders were worried, as was Lloyd. The experienced officers knew that the longer their troops remained in such conditions, the greater their ability to fight would be impaired. But Lloyd's sense of humour, known and appreciated throughout the brigade, provided the troops with some amusement. One morning, a Japanese artillery shell dropped just outside Lloyd's shelter but failed to explode in the soft mud. The brigadier summoned his batman, tapped the side with his walking stick and said, "Bury the bloody thing." The batman did so, proving that he was more scared of Lloyd than he was of the shell. The story went quickly around the brigade and gave the troops something to grin about.

The Australians were still suffering from being below the enemy, who held the ridges above the gorge. On the night of October 27/28, the 2/3rd Battalion and the 2/2nd Battalion were in close contact with the Japanese, while the 2/1st and Lloyd's headquarters remained in the rear. Japanese patrols had pushed forward during the night and were playing havoc with

FIGHTING THE FEVER

The Australian Army in New Guinea faced an enormous threat other than the Japanese infantry teeming over the jungled mountains towards Port Moresby. Tropical disease caused more casualties among the Australians than the armed enemy, and the soaring heat and humidity as well as continual rain severely affected all men fighting in the region.

Malaria was the biggest danger, being the most widespread infectious disease in the world and endemic to large areas of New Guinea. Swampy coastal lowlands, drenched by heavy rainfall, became huge breeding grounds for the carrier of the malaria parasite, the *Anopheles* mosquito. The female of the species was the insect responsible for infecting humans.

In wartime this debilitating and sometimes lethal disease had the potential to decimate the fighting strength of an army in the field. By 1942 the Australians had encountered malaria in Queensland and in the Mediterranean, the Middle East and Malaya, but New Guinea presented an even greater challenge for malaria control. In December 1942 malaria around the marshy coastland of Milne Bay escalated to epidemic proportions. Within weeks 5,000 cases were treated out of a troop strength of 16,000. Between October 1942 and April 1943, malarial cases in New Guinea Force totalled 20,272 compared to a battle casualty figure of 6,154 for the same period. In early 1943 another epidemic struck the battle-weary soldiers in the swamps around Buna and Gona, where many were already weakened by other tropical diseases such as dengue fever and dysentery.

Malaria is a distressing and incapacitating condition. After incubating in the liver, the parasite multiplies in the bloodstream causing the sufferer severe bouts of fever. Teeth-chattering chills last up to an hour as the body temperature rises as high as 40 degrees Celsius. The fever rages from four to eight hours with extreme headaches, vomiting, diarrhoea, and rapid breathing and pulse succeeded by profuse sweating as the temperature returns to normal. These attacks recur in cycles of two to four days. If the strain of parasite is particularly virulent, or the case complicated by other infectious diseases, the patient

To destroy breeding grounds for malaria-bearing mosquitoes, young native boys are conscripted to dig channels and drain waterlogged swampland near Port Moresby.

can die. Relapses of the disease are common at unpredictable intervals.

The battle against the disease-bearing mosquito took several forms. Anti-malarial units assigned to high-risk areas supervised the draining of swamps and canalising of streams to stop stagnant water collecting. Breeding grounds were sprayed with oil and chemical powder to suffocate larvae, but as the mosquito population burgeoned dispensers of compressed-gas insecticide known as freon "bombs" and aerial DDT spraying were used.

In 1942, Allied stocks of the standard anti-malarial drug, quinine, were running low because the Dutch East Indies island of Java, producer of 90 per cent of the world's supply of

quinine, was under Japanese occupation. With the loss of the drug to the enemy, Allied researchers had to test alternative synthetic suppressants to conserve their quinine supplies. The Australian Army's anti-malarial research unit in Cairns, experimenting with different types and dosages, found the drug atebrin able to control massive infection with hardly any toxic reaction.

The curse of malaria plagued the army for the entire New Guinea campaign. The disease sapped the Australian forces' fighting strength, but the hard work and dedication of Australian medical officers, scientists and researchers finally beat the malarial fever that almost destroyed all hope of victory in the Pacific War.

Major General George Vasey, a talented and colourful brigadier in Greece, took command of 7th Division in New Guinea in October 1942, soon winning the troops' affection.

Allied communications by cutting telephone lines between the companies. In much of the area visibility was down to 10 metres or less, yet from dawn on October 28 the Australians were fighting right along their front. The official historian called the battle a "grim game of blindman's buff."

Two companies of the 2/3rd Battalion now attacked from the left into the right flank of the Japanese positions. The Australian assault was preceded by a hail of hand grenades fired from rifles; it was the closest they could get to artillery fire. The two companies then attacked together, Lieutenant Bruce MacDougal commanding one of the platoons in the melee. "We sailed into them firing from the hip," he said. "The forward scouts were knocked out, but the men went on steadily, advancing from tree to tree until we were right through their outlying posts and into the central position. Suddenly the Japanese began to run out. They dropped their weapons and stumbled through the thick bush down the slope, squealing like frightened animals. In a minute or two, the survivors had disappeared into the bush." The key in the battle had been turned.

The next morning, the Australians buried more than 50 Japanese; some of the dead were wearing Australian wrist watches. "Before this Eora Creek fight the men had been saying the Japanese wouldn't run," said MacDougal. "Eora Creek proved he would."

Japanese resistance at Eora Creek had now ended. During the night of October 28/29, they slipped away to the next defensive position on the high ground between Oivi and Gorari, the withdrawal being conducted with great tactical skill. General Horii opted to fight at the points where he would have the greater advantage.

With the Japanese on the run, a great irony befell Major General Allen — he was removed from command of his beloved troops right at the peak of this success. Blamey, acting on demand of MacArthur, signalled him on October 27: "Consider that you have had sufficiently prolonged tour in forward area. General Vasey will arrive Myola by air morning October 28.

On arrival you will hand over command to him and return to Port Moresby for tour of duty in this area."

Allen replied: "It is regretted that it has been found necessary to relieve me at this juncture especially since the situation is improving daily and I feel the worst is behind us." Ever concerned about his soldiers, Allen added: "I would have preferred to have remained here until my troops had also been relieved."

Blamey had once again capitulated to the American general, who was still 2,500 kilometres away in Brisbane. Allen said later, "It was not necessary to urge me or the troops under my command to capture Kokoda. We were more anxious to get there than he was. It was a considerable hardship living and fighting in that country. Had I pressed the troops harder than I was doing at this stage, the operation could have resulted in failure to reach the objective and an unnecessary loss of life."

Major General George Vasey, sent forward to replace Allen as commander of the 7th Division, was known in the AIF as "Bloody George". It was a justly deserved nickname. As a brigadier in Greece he issued one of the most famous orders in the history of the Australian Army: "Here you... well are and here you ... well stay. And if any ... German gets between your post and the next, turn your ... Bren around and shoot him up the ..."

Vasey wasted no time communicating his vigour and personality to his soldiers. He took formal command on the morning of October 29, the morning after the Japanese had abandoned the Eora Creek delaying position. "The enemy is beaten," Vasey said. "Give him no rest and we will annihilate him. It is only a matter of a day or two. Tighten your belts and push on."

The soldiers certainly had to tighten their belts. Despite the capture of another dropping ground at Alola, the supply situation was still critical; virtually every soldier on the Kokoda Trail was going hungry.

The capture of Eora Creek gave Vasey not only an extra dropping ground, but also an extra axis on which to advance. Here the track diverged. On the left, or western fork, Vasey sent the 25th Brigade; on the right, through Missima, the 16th Brigade. But the 25th Brigade, which had been in the mountains longer than the 16th, was now almost exhausted, the men worn out by the driving torrential rain, the bitter cold at night, and the burden of up to five days' rations, when they could be obtained, a water bottle, a rifle, and up to 150 rounds of heavy .303 rifle ammunition. Despite the best efforts of the native carriers, the infantrymen on the Kokoda Trail were still beasts of burden. Frequently a day's hard march found the unit bivouacked less than two kilometres from the previous camp.

On the right, however, the fresher 16th Brigade was bouncing ahead, still without seeing any Japanese and still short of food, although many were lucky enough to get a hot meal on the last night of October. Such events were so infrequent that they were remembered and often noted in battalion war diaries. Now as the Australians entered areas that had been opened into garden patches for the nearby villagers, meagre rations could be supplemented with green bananas and

pawpaws. For most, it was their first fresh food since leaving Port Moresby weeks before.

From Missima the Australian patrols could see Kokoda, the village which had assumed such importance during the previous months. The platoon commander, Lieutenant A.N. Black, had patrolled cautiously forward along the western track and found that the Japanese had left two days before. So Kokoda was occupied by a platoon of the 2/31st Battalion on the morning of November 1. Before last light, Brigadier Eather had his advance headquarters in the village. The engineers, moving well forward, quickly inspected the airfield and reported that with two days' work, aircraft could land with urgently needed supplies and return with the ill and wounded.

On the day that the Australians had entered Kokoda, taking control of the top of the Owen Stanleys and finally ensuring Port Moresby's safety from an overland invasion, General MacArthur was pondering his plans for the Allies' drive on Buna. As well as the Kokoda Trail, his right flank was clear because of the Australian victory at Milne Bay. His air power was increasing almost daily. And his plan for outflanking New Guinea's mountains was under way.

Two battalions of Australia's 18th Brigade at Milne Bay were sent up the northeast coast to secure the seaward flank and the settlement of Wanigela with its airstrip. Soldiers of America's 32nd Division were marched from Kapa Kapa on the coast south of Port Moresby via Jaure towards the Wairopi area. It was a terrible march over some of the harshest ridges in the Owen Stanleys, the troops trudging through continual rain, their strength sapped with every step upwards and every drop down. Another team of U.S. 32nd Division soldiers were flown into Wanigela, intending to march from there to Buna while being supplied from the sea. They struck massive and impenetrable swamps, however, and were eventually shuttled around the coast to Pongani, where they finally grouped in early November. Nearby, at Fasari, was another excellent airstrip; both fields now

facilitated the rescue of the Americans from their debilitating trek across the mountains.

The Allied airforces had recently increased their transport capability, and the U.S. troops were the first to benefit. The arrival of more aircraft also meant that the cooks in the Australian infantry battalions still on the Kokoda Trail could now serve up something more palatable than the eternal diet of bully beef, broken biscuits and cold water. However, for many soldiers, the immediate effect of eating such delicacies as sugar, milk and tinned fruit was physically upsetting.

The 2/2nd missed out on the supply of fresh food. Urged on by an increasingly impatient Vasey, it led the 16th Brigade advance and began the pursuit of the Japanese back over the Kokoda Trail. On the morning of November 3, as the 2/2nd Battalion moved out of Kobara village to the junction of the track from Kokoda, they were met by the senior staff officer in Vasey's headquarters, Colonel Charles Spry, who had moved forward to talk with the 16th's commander Brigadier Lloyd. Although the troops were moving cautiously, the 2/2nd had not met any Japanese for four or five days. The advance guard for the battalion, "B" Company was clearing both sides of the track, but too slowly for the aggressive Lloyd. Impatient with the slow progress, Lloyd and Spry moved ahead past elements of the leading company until both senior officers were in front of the forward scouts. The 2/2nd's Captain C.H. Hodge wrote later: "Suddenly a burst of enemy automatic and rifle-fire rang out. What an exodus! The other ranks of brigade headquarters became keen to regain their correct places in the column. The party was led by 'Spag', the brigadier's cook, and as he left his yams and sweet potatoes carried in a bucket were sent flying in all directions."

Lieutenant Colonel C.R.V. "Boss" Edgar, commanding the 2/2nd, was perturbed that, instead of having his forward scouts in contact with the enemy, he had the brigade commander, the senior divisional staff officer and their small protection party under fire.

Edgar quickly ordered a company to move around each side of the track and relieve this potentially embarrassing situation. Losing a staff officer would be bad enough; losing a brigadier as well would be sheer carelessness.

The incident involving Lloyd and Spry was typical of the current Japanese efforts. Small parties of determined Japanese could impose considerable delay on the Australian advance and thus buy time for the defenders around Buna and Gona. The Japanese technique was simple enough: with a mountain-gun and machine-gun, they would fire on the oncoming Australians, forcing them to deploy and prepare for an attack. As the Australian attack was being prepared, however, the Japanese would attempt to slip away, only to repeat the manoeuvre a little further down the track.

The Australians, by now becoming more aware of the Japanese tactics, tried a counter of their own. As soon as one company was held up astride a track, another would begin a wide encircling movement through the bush, and try to get behind the Japanese. This drill was common enough at platoon level, but never before had a battalion commander committed around 60 men in a company to such a move without knowing more about the detail of the Japanese positions. In the 2/2nd Battalion, such tactics produced considerable successes and the Australians came closer and closer to the Japanese main defensive positions on the high ground from Oivi to Gorari.

By this time, however, the 2/2nd Battalion was down to about 300 men. Diarrhoea and dysentery were rife, and just about every man was suffering with high temperatures and harsh hacking coughs from the rain and the cold. Although the remainder of the Australian battalions closed up behind the 2/2nd, nearing Japan's defensive positions, the attackers were not yet strong enough to strike a decisive blow. Here too, the Australians struck enemy bunkers for the first time, dug in on high ground and containing the Japanese medium machine-gun known to its foes as the ''Woodpecker'', and each protected by lighter machine-guns and

Trudging along a boggy track, walking wounded return from fighting around Oivi to a dressing station. By November 8, the veterans of 16th Brigade had a battle casualty toll of 386.

rifles. For the first time now, however, the Australians had mortar ammunition in large quantities, thanks to the opening of the Kokoda airfield. The odds were gradually turning in favour of the Australian troops.

Oivi was a major obstacle to the Australian pursuit. The Japanese positions had to be cleared, and the defenders killed so that they could not withdraw to fight again further down the track. To do so, Vasey had to put in a major attack, requiring several days' careful planning and a longer build-up of essential materials such as rifle and mortar ammunition. From the administrative point of view, Vasey had one priceless advantage. The security of the Kokoda base and its airfield gave him much more flexibility and opportunity than Allen had ever had. He could now develop an attack using both his available brigades.

The 16th Brigade was in contact with the enemy in front of Oivi, so Vasey ordered his men to maintain the pressure. The 25th Brigade, restocked with supplies from Kokoda, was ordered to swing around south of the Japanese position and cut them off from the Kumusi River. Such a movement was potentially dangerous; had the Japanese launched a counter-attack against the 16th Brigade positions in any force while the 25th Brigade was moving, Vasey would have had no reserve to plug any holes appearing in his front. It was also the first time in the war that such a movement at brigade level was made against the Japanese; it had not been attempted elsewhere, either in Malaya or in Burma. Although it was the kind of movement that MacArthur was urging from the comfort of his air-conditioned hotel in Brisbane, it was of such complexity that it could only be performed by highly trained and well-disciplined troops.

While the movement was going on, Vasey was able to get some tactical air support from American fighter-bombers in place of artillery. But this close air support was something of a mixed advantage, Captain Hodge recalled: "We had been supported by them once before at Eora Creek, but they had frightened us more than

they had the Japanese. Now we were to have help again. They bombed the feature with reasonable accuracy, and strafed Oivi village behind. The Japs, however, were so well dug in that we doubted whether the air support would be effective. In any case, the Yanks didn't hit us on this occasion."

They did, however, rain their bombs on the 2/3rd, whose signallers were responsible for sending up target rockets to assist the Americans' aim. But the updraught from the mountains carried the plumes of signal smoke back over the Australians who copped the results — there were, however, no casualties.

As the 16th Brigade kept up the pressure on the Japanese at Oivi by intense patrolling, the 25th Brigade moved around to take the defenders from behind and cut their communications. The brigade set out in drenching rain, but at last the going was good on clearly defined tracks. By November 8 the 2/31st, the forward troops of the 25th Brigade, were pressing against the Japanese defenders at Gorari. The 2/25th Battalion now swung around to the right and came in against the Japanese opposite to the 2/31st. It was a classic pincer operation.

Now the battle developed into a solid slugging match as the Japanese attempted to fight their way out of a trap that had been cleverly laid. The Australians prepared for the stroke that would take them clear of this delaying position, but for the men of the 2/33rd it was a case of being caught in the middle as the Japanese realised their main defences at Oivi were sandwiched between Australians pressing from the west and the south. If the 2/33rd Battalion should be dislodged from its precarious hold then the operation would be jeopardised: the battalion simply had to hold on.

At the time, its strength was down to 16 officers and 271 other ranks. On the morning of November 10 its patrols reported that two companies of Japanese were just 400 metres away to the west and preparing for an assault. All that day Japanese gunners pounded the Australian position with mortar and mountain-

On a makeshift bridge constructed hastily by Australian engineers in November 1942, troops cross the Kumusi River at Wairopi, the site of a steel-cable suspension bridge used by the Japanese and demolished by Allied aircraft.

gun fire, each shelling followed by a charge by their infantry. These desperate assaults came in on the 2/33rd positions from the west and then the northwest as the Japanese fought tenaciously to dislodge the equally stubborn Australian defenders.

On that terrible November 10, the men of "D" Company of the 2/33rd suffered grievously; a Japanese 3-inch mountain-gun was firing into their position at almost point-blank range. Warrant Officer Bill Crooks thought the situation at one stage was just "touch and go". A few men began running back, but one of the corporals was sent to bring them in. Later the company commander moved among some of the more demoralised troops with his pistol drawn, threatening to shoot any more who moved. Crooks wrote: "The sight of stricken comrades, some of whom were being blown to pieces before their eyes, was demoralising to already operationally weak men. There were few such cases during this campaign where units had to face such a situation, and suffer so much in such a short incident. Cannon at open sights and no trenches just do not make men brave." Sadly, the 2/33rd's casualties in the last two days were serious; it had lost five men killed and 27 wounded. Three other battalions had lost 40 men killed and 100 wounded.

To the east, the 2/1st Battalion of the 16th Brigade managed to relieve some of the Japanese pressure on the 2/33rd. Now, too, the 2/31st and the 2/25th were able to move cautiously around the Japanese positions and complete the encirclement. During the night of November 10/11, the men of the 2/1st Battalion repulsed attack after attack, as the Japanese fought desperately to get through to the east of the 2/33rd. By the morning of November 11, however, the shelling on the 2/33rd had stopped and the Japanese had begun to flee back towards their defences at Buna.

As they did so, the Australians moved forward from both the north and the south onto the enemy's escape route, firing with rifles only so as to avoid the risk of hitting each other. The sound of the battle soon died away, and although the forest valley had been a fearsome killing ground on the morning of November 11, by noon it seemed that the bulk of the Japanese had gone. By nightfall, their defences around Oivi-Gorari had been broken; the heavy fighting around the 2/1st position the previous night had been from the main Japanese forces around Oivi as they had pulled back.

The withdrawal was skilfully executed. The Japanese had linked vines between trees along the route and placed hooded candles to help their troops find the way. Now some of the Australians rested while others took up the pursuit to the Kumusi River and the wire-rope

bridge which spanned it. The responsibility for the pursuit was given to the 2/31st Battalion, which had been less heavily affected by the fighting around Oivi-Gorari. It reached the river on the 13th, only to discover from locals that the Japanese had crossed the night before. Some Japanese had tried to reach the coast by rafting down the swiftly flowing waterway, but many of these rafts were shot by patrols of the Papuan Infantry Battalion operating on the coastline. Among the casualties was the Japanese force commander, General Horii, who drowned when his raft capsized.

The Australian engineers rapidly threw another bridge across the Kumusi to supplement the footbridge and flying foxes. "The scene at the river bank," wrote the 16th Brigade diarist, "was reminiscent of an old English fair or Irish market day. Battalions of heavily laden troops in their mud-stained jungle shirts and slacks, carrier lines with the natives gaily caparisoned in bright coloured lap-laps, bedecked with flowers and sprigs of shrubs stuck jauntily in leather bracelets, all mingled as they waited their turn to cross."

With the Australians over the Kumusi River, and the Japanese withdrawn to the Buna-Gona area, the fight for the Owen Stanleys was over. In four months the Australians had lost 625 killed and more than 1,000 wounded on the Kokoda Trail, the heaviest losses occurring in the earlier days of the campaign. And for every battle casualty, perhaps two or three others were hospitalised through illness or disease. With Kokoda behind them the worst may now have seemed over, but more bitter fighting now lay ahead as the Australians went on to the tropical waters of the north Papuan coast.

"May the mothers of Australia, when they offer up a prayer, mention those impromptu angels with their fuzzy wuzzy hair"

A wounded Digger is given a light by a Papuan stretcher-bearer. Thousands of natives aided the Allied war effort in New Guinea.

Bringing supplies forward, barefoot carriers pass a tired Australian unit in the long, tough trek over the Finisterre Ranges.

CARRYING THE WHITE MAN'S BURDEN

When war came to Papua and the Australian Mandated Territory of New Guinea, only about 8,000 foreigners including Australian planters, miners, traders, missionaries and administrators lived among an estimated one-and-a-half million native peoples. As thousands of Allied and Japanese soldiers began to invade this remote and primitive world in 1942, the natives' lives were tragically disrupted, and they were often brutally exploited.

They were dragged into a terrifying war not of their own making. A pre-war colonial native labour market had created a pool of more than 45,000 indentured labourers, and in June 1942 they were conscripted to the service of the Australian Army. Natives acted as supply carriers over the Owen Stanley Range and the Finisterre Range to the north. As stretcher-bearers they evacuated the wounded. As scouts they trekked along overgrown jungle trails. They worked on road, airfield and barrack construction and anti-malarial swamp clearance, and, as well, they operated as informants. They were also put into uniform, and by war's end three native infantry battalions totalling 2,500 natives were in the field. They played an indispensable part in the jungle offensive. One Australian soldier laconically observed: "No boongs, no battle."

The Australian soldiers may have seemed paternalistic in their relations with the Papuans, but their bond of gratitude to their "dark-skinned brothers" was always genuine. It was most famously expressed in a poem written on the Kokoda Trail by Sapper H. Beros and published in the Australian press. The poem concluded: "May the mothers of Australia when they offer up a prayer, mention those impromptu angels with their fuzzy wuzzy hair." The title "Fuzzy Wuzzy Angels" stuck as an affectionate name.

Not all natives were angelically loyal to the Australians. Survival often depended on capitulation to whichever army occupied a tribe's territory. Intimidated by Japanese who bombed and burned their villages, many tribesmen served them as scouts, carriers and spies.

The Japanese captured and killed many civilians and Allied soldiers with native help. As a result, a series of kangaroo court trials ordered by senior Australian commanders and conducted by local magistrates between July 1943 and August 1944 ended in the hanging of at least 50 Papuan "collaborators". A number of summary executions also occurred.

Those natives who did serve the Australians paid a heavy toll. Overworked and underfed, carriers succumbed in alarming numbers to pneumonia and tropical disease. The heavy drain on village manpower seriously disrupted village agriculture and life. Yet, despite a promised fee of 10 shillings for each Japanese soldier taken alive or dead, the Australian government never compensated the natives for their contribution or losses. Many Australian soldiers pleaded the Fuzzy Wuzzy Angels' case, but to no avail. At least the Diggers themselves would never forget them.

A native stretcher-bearer comforts Private F.A. Matthews of the 2/2nd Battalion with a drink of water before the wounded soldier is evacuated from the battle zone by plane. A broad palm leaf, stuck in the ground, provides shade from the sun.

Left: Surefooted stretcher-bearers use walking sticks to steady their dizzying descent from Shaggy Ridge, in the Finisterre Range, to the Faria River valley below. Long treks left the natives' shoulders raw and bloody. Above: The surface of an RAAF airstrip is rolled flat using native labour.

Three native soldiers and Private N.V. Hooper of the 2/8th Battalion take cover while pinned down by enemy fire out on patrol around Wewak.

An estimated 85 Papuan and New Guinean soldiers and members of the Royal Papuan Constabulary were killed in action and 201 wounded.

2

THE BEACHHEAD BATTLES

Prepared for a bloody fight, the Japanese dug in on Papua's north coast. The Australians paid dearly in their assaults on Gona and Sanananda while American troops were slaughtered at Buna. But, with tanks and fresh troops, the Allies smashed all three strongholds.

Japan had suffered heavily on the Kokoda Trail, but its soldiers' withdrawal to Buna had been conducted with great skill and the survivors had pulled back in reasonably good condition. Their defensive positions were well sited and they were adequately supplied from the sea. The Japanese knew that they simply had to hold on. Their position stretched for about 70 kilometres, from Gona in the northwest to Cape Endaiadere in the southeast. Although their three main defensive positions at Gona, at Sanananda Point, and in the Buna area were independent of the other, the flanks and gaps between them were well protected, and communications between them were good. Reinforcements could be easily deployed and switched as threats developed.

In each position the Japanese had prepared hundreds of coconut-log bunkers, each containing a medium machine-gun, and each capable of firing in protection of its neighbours. The bunkers were covered with earth and vegetation, which grew quickly in the climate to provide excellent camouflage. Each position had depth, ranging from a few hundred metres

Sculptor Ray Ewer's bronze group "End Of Trail, Buna" captures the physical strain of the Owen Stanleys trek.

to more than a kilometre, so that an attacker had to do much more than merely penetrate an outer ring of defences. Long and arduous fights could be expected for each objective, and each bunker had to be pinpointed and attacked while its neighbours were being tackled. Then the whole process would have to begin again. In all, the Japanese had about 9,000 men in a solid fortress, including about 4,000 reinforcements landed in October and November.

By comparison the Allies were in poor shape. The Australian 7th Division, consisting of the 16th, 21st and 25th Brigades, had been through months of hard fighting on the Kokoda Trail. The 21st Brigade and the militia units of the 30th Brigade who had met the Japanese first were back in Port Moresby awaiting reinforcements. The 16th and 25th Brigades were seriously understrength and worn out.

New to the country, the United States 32nd Division was inexperienced, poorly trained and far from ready for combat, with one of its regiments in terrible condition from its arduous haul over the Jaure track. Then there were the Americans who had been flown over the mountains: when the Australian 2/2nd Battalion first met them they thought their new allies looked fresh and healthy. Major J.W. Dunlop wrote that the Americans ''had more cigarettes than they could smoke, though they were unaccountably short of food. They were most generous with their cigarettes. They had, they said, no idea that the AIF had ended the inland campaign and was already on the northern side of the Owen Stanleys.''

Blamey had planned for a quick offensive against the Japanese at Buna and Gona, but now MacArthur dallied, insisting that ''at least 10 days' supply of food and appropriate amount of ammunition and medical supplies'' should be built up for the Buna attack. He had finalised his operational plans on November 3, choosing mid-month to go in. New Guinea Force's orders were for the U.S. 32nd Division to capture the Buna-Cape Endaiadere sector, and for the 7th Australian Division to capture Gona and Sanananda.

The Americans were moving on Buna in a three-pronged attack: the 128th Regiment had flown into Wanigela and, with the Australian 2/6th Independent Company, was moving northwest along the coast; the 126th Regiment was moving from Fasari north to Pongani; and another battalion was moving north, across country, from Jaure. Within the Australian forces, the 16th Brigade was to cross the Kumusi River and advance via Popondetta and Soputa along the inland road to Sanananda, and the 25th Brigade was to head for Gona.

The terrain had changed drastically from the tangled mountains and ravines of the Owen Stanleys. The hinterland consisted of dense jungles thick with vines and undergrowth which impeded rapid movement. Patches of shoulder-high and razor-sharp kunai grass added to the obstacles. The coastline was flat and swampy, broken by coconut plantations and numerous creeks running down to the sea.

While the Allied forces made their way through such inhospitable country, closing up on their enemy on three separate fronts, MacArthur's plans elsewhere were in limbo. The fighting was bitter on Guadalcanal, and for three days beginning on November 12 a vicious naval battle ensued — the Americans eventually triumphed, destroying a large enemy convoy carrying reserves. Japan was now virtually powerless to reinforce Guadalcanal, and the advantage swung towards the U.S. forces there, who were increasingly stronger and readying themselves for a major Solomons offensive.

The Allies' emphasis now shifted back to the New Guinea mainland. Major General Edwin Harding, commanding the American 32nd Division, planned a two-axes attack at Cape Endaiadere on November 19, while on the same day the 16th Australian Brigade also struck the Japanese at Soputa, and the 25th Brigade was held up outside Gona village.

The Americans thought that Buna village was easily within their grasp, but they were to be horribly mistaken. Nothing seemed to go right for these fresh but green troops. After the 126th Regiment was switched from Harding's command to Vasey's, the U.S. commander was now forced to put in just one battalion against the Japanese defences at Buna village, and another battalion along a track bordered by impenetrable swamps lying between the two main approaches to the village. Torrential rain beat down on the Americans as they headed towards the Japanese, who had been well warned by the Allies' preparations in the area. They shocked the attackers with their excellent fields of fire and snipers placed everywhere; the Americans were beaten back, some troops blazing off all their ammunition at targets they could only imagine.

In Port Moresby, General MacArthur's early optimism vanished. He began to apply pressure to his subordinates, telling Blamey, who was still in New Guinea, that his forces had to attack, urging that "all columns will be driven through regardless of losses." On November 21, MacArthur told Harding: "Take Buna today at all costs."

But around Buna the confusion was immense. American aircraft attacked what they thought were Japanese positions — instead they bombed their own men, aggravating an already deteriorating morale problem. As well, with constant rain and heat, a poor supply system, and the stubborn Japanese, discipline was becoming a problem in the American units. Their soldiers were simply refusing to move; others had dropped their weapons and run away. Major General Vasey, who visited the American 126th Regiment, wrote to Blamey that the situation remained unsatisfactory. The U.S. soldiers, Vasey said, had maintained a "masterly inactivity".

On November 25, MacArthur, Blamey and Herring met in Port Moresby at Government House to discuss this lack of progress by the American troops at Buna. MacArthur suggested bringing the U.S. 41st Division from Australia, but Blamey replied that he would rather have more Australians, "because he knew they would fight." Both Blamey and Herring expanded on reports MacArthur had already received about the poor morale and discipline of

the 32nd Division. It was, wrote American General George C. Kenney, the SWPA's Allied Air Forces Commander, a "bitter pill for MacArthur to swallow."

By November 30, two weeks after the attack had begun, the Americans had suffered nearly 500 battle casualties and probably three times that number in non-battle casualties, but they had not made one single penetration of the Japanese defences. MacArthur now summoned Lieutenant General R.L. Eichelberger from Rockhampton to Port Moresby. "A real leader," MacArthur told Eichelberger, "could take these same men and capture Buna." Eichelberger was to go to Buna, relieve Harding and all the other unaggressive American officers or, said MacArthur, "I will relieve them and you too." MacArthur paced up and down the veranda of Government House, turned to Eichelberger, and said intensely: "Go out there, Bob, and take Buna or don't come back alive." The next day, however, MacArthur mellowed his orders, promising Eichelberger that if he took Buna he would receive the American Distinguished Service Cross, a recommendation for a British honour and, the grandest prize of all, a prominent citation in press releases.

And so, with his 1 American Corps head-quarters, Eichelberger set about unscrambling the mess the Americans had created. One major obstacle to the Americans and the Australians was the system of bunkers the Japanese had built. Against such defences and their machine-guns, lightly armoured Allied infantry without flame throwers, rockets or tanks had little chance. There were tanks available at Milne Bay, but no method of getting them to the Buna battlefields, so Eichelberger opted to use the lightly armoured Bren-gun carriers as a substitute. These vehicles were not to perform the role usually given to tanks — of blasting infantry onto an objective — instead, they were simply to provide covering fire for an infantry assault. However, this task was too much, and the Bren-gun crews were shot to pieces. Buna remained firmly in Japanese hands.

At Gona, the Australians were also involved

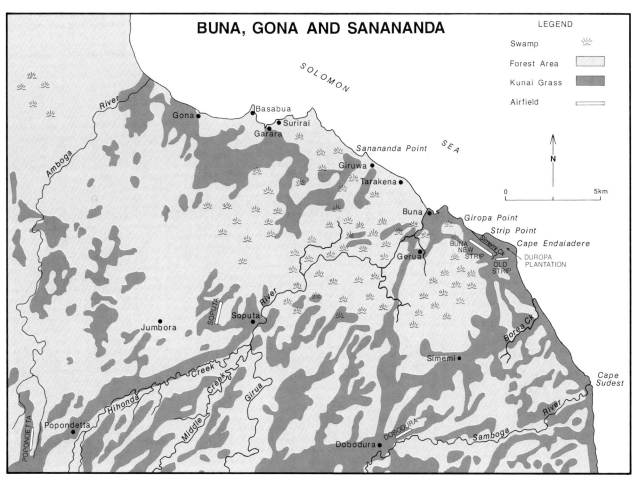

BUNA, GONA AND SANANANDA

LEGEND

Swamp

Forest Area

Kunai Grass

Airfield

SOLOMON SEA

Gona
Basabua
Surirai
Garara
Sanananda Point
Giruwa
Tarakena
Buna
Giropa Point
Strip Point
Cape Endaiadere
BUNA NEW STRIP
OLD STRIP
Gerua
DUROPA PLANTATION
Amboga River
Jumbora
Soputa
SOPUTA River
Girua River
Simemi
Borea Ck
Cape Sudest
Hihonda Creek
Middle Creek
Popondetta
POPONDETTA
Dobodura
DOBODURA
Samboga River

N

0   5km

During November 1942, assaults on Japanese defences at Gona, Buna and Sanananda cost the Allied forces heavy battle casualties, but by January 21, 1943, all three strongholds collapsed and enemy survivors fled north.

in a desperate struggle. The 25th Brigade, with the 2/33rd Battalion leading, had moved from Wairopi to the village of Jumbora without striking any Japanese in strength. Once again, the speed of the advance outstripped the supplies. The battalion paused to prepare a dropping ground and, on the orders of Brigadier Eather, to send one company forward to see if there were any Japanese in Gona. Not one company in the battalion was strong enough to do the job; instead 60 fit men from all the companies were selected and placed under the command of Captain Tom Clowes.

Moving out of their night camp just north of Jumbora at first light on November 18, by 11 am Clowes's men were within 1,200 metres of the sea, in sight of coconut palms on the shore and huts of the old mission station. Clowes halted his force and sent forward a small reconnaissance patrol under Lieutenant J. Elliott. As the Australians probed cautiously forward, Elliott's group came under fire, first from an isolated rifleman, and then

concentrated blasts of rifle and machine-guns. The 2/31st Battalion, pressing hard on the heels of Clowes's patrol, came forward and tried to attack from the right and left, but its attack was met with another fearsome hail of fire from the Japanese. As the night wore on, the 2/31st lost more than 30 of its men killed and wounded, including four company commanders. By early morning on November 20, the battered battalion had been forced to pull back through a protective screen established by Clowes's patrol. Although some of the men on the right of the attack had got forward almost to the huts of the village, the Japanese defences had been too well-prepared. The Australians were also handicapped by a lack of artillery fire to put down on the Japanese bunkers. Eather's brigade was now desperately short of supplies, and he postponed further attacks until they came. On November 21 the men were replenished with air-dropped food, ammunition, quinine and tobacco, so that the next day the tired troops summoned up their energy for another attack 57 on the Gona position. This time Eather used two battalions with a third in reserve about three kilometres south of the village. The 2/33rd began their moves in the morning, taking 18 killed and wounded. But it was the 2/31st that suffered terribly that day. As its men charged in against the Japanese bunkers they were met with a terrible intensity of fire from the front and the right, but the Australians kept going, cheering and yelling as they went, eventually reaching the forward Japanese pits. But they were not strong enough to push on; the attack had cost several young officers among 65 killed, wounded and missing. Once again, the Australians were forced to withdraw.

Not only the Japanese defence, but the scorching tropical climate began to waste the battalions. "In the unsheltered kunai, with its shimmering heat and still air, temperatures climbed to over 130 degrees Fahrenheit," reported Warrant Officer Crooks. "For already exhausted men the conditions were almost unbearable. Nearly all were running temperatures over 100, but such was the determination of the men that they did not report sick until the temperatures read 105-106."

Men began to wander around the kunai, muttering incoherently; two of the young platoon commanders had nearly a full-time job grabbing heat casualties and dunking them in shell-littered water holes to cool off.

It was clear now that the Japanese defenders at Gona were too strong and too well-prepared for the depleted 25th Brigade. At a solemn conference on the morning of November 24, Brigadier Eather discovered that his battalions were seriously understrength; he could do nothing more than contain the Japanese. Certainly he did not have enough men to break through and capture Gona. And he was worried about the possibility of a strong Japanese counter-attack which, if successful, might destroy the gains already made.

Those worst fears were realised at dusk on November 25 when the Japanese thrust fiercely back at the Australians. The weight of the enemy fell on the combined "A" and "D" company of the 2/33rd Battalion, whose battered groups had been merged to give them some power. Even so, they were down to only 40 men, as opposed to 80 to 100 in a full-strength rifle company. The commander, Lieutenant K. Power, sized up the situation quickly. He leapt to the edge of the trench and yelled, "Come on you Jap bastards, we're waiting for you. Battalion, fix bayonets and prepare to charge." Inspired by Power's example, the tired Australians began to fire through the kunai grass at the oncoming Japanese, and in the harsh tropical sun the enemy could see the glint of the Australian steel. By courage and bluff on the part of the Australians, the Japanese attack was broken off.

Now, for the Australians, the battle had changed, and they were forced to defend. That night they cut fire-lanes in the grass and coordinated the arcs of their machine-guns with the battalions nearby. From the sea, they could hear Japanese barges resupplying their troops in Gona. For the weary, starved Australians it was a fearful sound.

Vasey had another brigade, the 21st, to throw into the attack on Gona. It was commanded by Brigadier Ivan Dougherty, a pre-war militia officer who had led the 2/4th Battalion in the desert. He was a fine tactician with a keen and questioning mind; Vasey sent him forward to discuss the situation with Eather. There were two possible roles for Dougherty's brigade: to reinforce the 25th, then barely holding on at Gona; or to assist the 16th Brigade in its thrust against Sanananda.

"At no place did our strength appear to be sufficient to defeat the enemy," Dougherty wrote later. The brigadier decided that elimination of the enemy in front of Gona, with the cooperation of the 25th Brigade, was the most desirable course — a decision that was immediately reinforced when he saw how weary the 25th Brigade troops were after their ordeals of the previous months.

But Dougherty's own brigade was itself only about 1,000 men strong. It had met the Japanese

With heads bowed solemnly, 25th Brigade soldiers pray before their next assault on Japanese machine-gun nests and trench systems around Gona village. Repeated attacks across thick scrub and swampland were thrown back with heavy casualties.

earlier on the Kokoda Trail, suffered grievously and had not yet been fully reinforced. It flew into Popondetta, where General Herring, commanding New Guinea Force, had established his headquarters. Worried about the possibility of Japanese reinforcements arriving at the beachhead, HQ ordered an early attack, which Dougherty planned to make from the east while the 2/14th Battalion, supported by the 2/27th and an American airstrike, struck westwards along the coastline towards the Japanese. Even before it could get into position for this attack, however, the 2/14th was beaten back by murderous Japanese machine-gun fire from well-concealed positions. Then it was the turn of the 2/27th, which struck against the eastern side of the Japanese position on November 29. On the same day, the 2/14th tried again against the defences on the coast. Eather's hard-pressed 25th Brigade was called in to assist, while the militia 3rd Battalion and the 2/33rd pushed in from the south. Again it was to no avail.

But on November 30 after a hard struggle, the 2/14th managed to clear the coast between Gona and Basabua, where the Japanese had landed six months before. On that day, too, an attempt to reinforce the Japanese garrison at Gona by barges from Sanananda was beaten back off the beach by Australian patrols — at last the Diggers were beginning to make progress in reducing this fearsome fortress.

On December 1, Dougherty's brigade tried again to take the village of Gona. Once more it was beaten back, this time by concentrated Japanese counter-attacks. Dougherty's formation, understrength at the beginning, was being wasted further by the continual heavy fighting and the illnesses rife in the fetid coastal swamps. The fighting had devastated the young officers and NCOs, many of whom had been promoted from the ranks after their efforts in the Middle East. Now, in the close country, as they gave their orders and directions they were instantly recognisable and became targets for the ubiquitous Japanese snipers and machine-guns. The 2/14th was down to seven officers

and 152 other ranks on November 30, less than 20 per cent of its full strength.

Vasey was now worried about the extent of the Australian casualties at Gona; at one stage he thought about leaving a force to contain the Japanese there while moving on their positions at Sanananda. There was more than a hint of desperation amongst the Australian commanders as they shuffled weary troops around, looking for a means to crack the stubborn Japanese defenders. There was political pressure as well. Vasey wrote to one battalion commander who had complained about the heavy casualties: "Canberra must have news of a clean-up and have it quick or we will both go by the boot."

So far, most of the fighting had been done by the veteran AIF brigades. Early in December, Vasey received reinforcements in the form of the militia 30th Brigade. One of its battalions, the 39th, under the skilful and inspiring leadership of Lieutenant Colonel Ralph Honner, boosted Dougherty's troops around Gona. The other two militia battalions, the 49th which had been defending Port Moresby since the beginning of the Papuan campaign, and the combined 55th/53rd were sent to Sanananda to reinforce the 16th Brigade.

Again on December 6, Dougherty tried to dislodge the Japanese from Gona. The 39th Battalion attacked northwestward against the Japanese position, which had contracted into a short stretch of beach about 400 metres square, with the sea on the north, the 21st Brigade to the east and the 25th Brigade on the south and west. After the war, Ralph Honner wrote that his troops had seen the unpromising ground in front of the 2/16th and 2/27th Battalions "stretching flat and featureless to the northern Japanese positions near the beach. There was no adequate cover for daylight attack."

Honner's first attack bogged down after taking heavy casualties for no real gains. In one of the 39th's companies, 58 men were killed or wounded when smoke laid to mask the Australian movement served only to help conceal the Japanese positions. Another attack

ALLIES AT ODDS

Two American sailors enjoy a day out with their Australian sweethearts. The U.S. visitors were popular amongst the girls, but the murder of three Melbourne women by an American soldier in May 1942 temporarily tarnished the GIs' sex appeal.

To Australians at home and fighting abroad, American servicemen in Australia were both the darlings and the villains of World War II. The Allied war effort against Japan became based in Australia, and the numbers of Americans swelled. By early 1943 more than 250,000 were stationed in Brisbane, Melbourne, Sydney, Perth and in smaller towns.

Australians tried to make their visitors feel at home: Thanksgiving and American Independence Day were celebrated; newspapers covered American politics and sports; U.S. flags flew from public buildings; and the "Star Spangled Banner" often played in cinemas and on radio.

This fascination with the Yank was not shared by the Australian Army. Regarding the Americans as late-comers in both world wars, the Digger was resentful of the hero-worship the Yank attracted. Other factors increased the tension. United States troops were on much higher pay than Australians and, combined with a favourable exchange rate, the Yankee dollar began to monopolise just about every item in short supply, particularly liquor and tobacco. Prices on goods were driven up by the Yanks' excessive spending power. Local taxi drivers, shopkeepers and restauranteurs began to favour Americans in expectation of big tips.

American soldiers also enjoyed superior living conditions to the Diggers. The Australians ate tinned food, mutton, and had small beer allowances. The Yanks were lavished with beef steaks, ice-cream, copious quantities of beer and cigarettes, glossy magazines and visits from big-name entertainers.

With such luxuries to spare, American servicemen easily attracted Australian women. The number of marriages between U.S. soldiers and Australian girls escalated and by January 1945 more than 10,000 war brides and fiancees were waiting to be reunited with their husbands in America. Many Diggers were not impressed, and some attacked any GI seen with an Australian girl. Resentment led to brawls, stabbings and even riots. One fracas, sparked by clashes with U.S. military police on November 26, 1942, and known as the "Battle of Brisbane", turned into two days of attacks and mob brawls. Mass fights also occurred in Sydney, Perth and Melbourne, where in February 1943 a riot broke out involving 2,000 soldiers and civilians.

En masse, the American servicemen placed a great strain on Australia's hospitality and sense of gratitude. A poem in *Smith's Weekly* newspaper expressed the local frustration: "To the Yanks: They saved us from the Japs, perhaps. But at the moment the place is too Yankful for us to be sufficiently thankful."

Another "Stars and Stripes" comes off the production line at a Melbourne factory in June 1942. Offices and public buildings in the state capital cities all flew American flags for Independence Day on July 4.

During a wartime rally in Sydney, Australian and American troops march together in a show of Allied unity. The American uniform was widely considered smarter than the traditional Australian khaki — much to the Diggers' chagrin.

The popular Sunday Telegraph comic strip "Bluey and Curley" takes a lighthearted jab at a Digger's sexual jealousy. Many Australian soldiers were grieved and angered by the Yanks' success with Aussie girls.

Being served by friendly Australians, one U.S. soldier appears dubious about the food. Despite attempts to make Yanks feel at home, mutual cultural ignorance increased tensions between Americans and Australians.

Brigadier Ivan Dougherty boards a reconnaissance aircraft in New Guinea. He threw his 21st Brigade into the Gona offensive to support the exhausted 25th Brigade.

Edgell, gained the swamp line which protected the enemy's southern defences. As his section moved forward, a Japanese machine-gun opened fire and Edgell was wounded twice in the right arm. He quickly changed his Owen machine-carbine to the left arm and, charging onwards, took out the enemy gun and killed the three men manning it. Behind Edgell, his platoon commander saw what was happening and pushed forward until he struck an enemy strong-post on the right of the rough track. Single-handedly Plater stalked the post, killing its officer and four soldiers and capturing the machine-gun. Over the next four hours Plater led a series of platoon attacks, always putting himself at the lead with his Owen and grenades. Just on dusk, Plater was shot through the shoulder when he was dressing the wound of one of his corporals who had been shot. The young officer finished his bandaging, went back to his platoon and personally led another attack before being carried out on a litter.

That night, as the Australians clung on to the hard-won swampy ground, it rained. The water rose from the swamp line, and Ralph Honner recalled that the only men not in the water were the wounded, for whom table-high platforms had been built. "All through that deluged night I sat, tree-backed, upon a log to lift my face above the spreading sewer. When the flood receded, latrines and new-dug graves and weapons pits looked all alike."

But now the Japanese defenders at Gona were just about spent. Under the cover of the rain and darkness, a party tried to break out to Sanananda, but they were intercepted and shot to pieces in the darkness. The next morning the Australians moved in and, after desperate hand-to-hand fighting with the last of the defenders, finally captured the village late in the morning of November 9. "Gona's gone," a jubilant Honner signalled. It was a significant victory, for elsewhere along the front the campaign had slowed to a bitter slogging match, almost a war of attrition in the style of the First World War's Western Front.

When Gona was captured, the Australians

by the 39th, planned for the following day, was cancelled by Honner when preliminary air strikes fell not on the Japanese but in the Australian rear areas.

Now Dougherty's brigade was less than the strength of one full battalion; the Australian brigadier had just one more chance to attack this seemingly intractable position, and Vasey gave him 250 rounds of artillery for the attack. Under the cover of this shelling and the battalion's own mortars, the 39th would attack from the south, while the 2/16th and the 2/27th came in from the east.

The artillery and mortar fire dropped on the Japanese positions for 15 minutes. Honner's soldiers watched as the Japanese put on their gas respirators; the bombardment churned up the stench of their comrades' rotting corpses. "Many of our battle-hardened veterans fighting their way forward over that polluted ground, were unable to face their food," Honner wrote. "It was sickening to breathe, let alone eat."

As the 39th moved up into this attack, their leading platoon was commanded by a young Duntroon officer, Lieutenant Ron Plater. One of Plater's section commanders, Corporal R.G.

Grim-faced American soldiers bring in wounded from Buna in early December 1942. After two weeks of fighting, the U.S. 32nd Division lost 492 men in battle and gained no ground.

buried 638 Japanese dead; and many more were lost in the swamps and bush. The Australians had lost 750 killed and wounded, about half the strength of the units involved. It had been a high price. The fighting, however, was not over for the 39th Battalion, for there were still Japanese to the west near the mouth of the Kumusi River. It fell to Honner's men to make sure they did not get back to Gona, and a company pushed west of the village to secure the area.

The 39th, arriving late in the battle, had played one of the decisive roles. It had fought as well as the battle-experienced AIF battalions, yet some of its reinforcements had the barest of training. After Gona, Honner's intelligence officer was asked by one young soldier, "Please sir, would you show me how this gun works? I've never had one of these before."

Honner looked up at the weapon. "It was the ordinary .303 that every recruit cuts his teeth on," Honner recalled, looking at the lad in wonderment. "He had played his part with a fixed bayonet and a stout heart in all his section's battles through the jungle filth, the swamp miasma and the fetid stench, too proud to proclaim his ignorance of the functioning of a rifle bolt to those friends who had accepted him as one of themselves."

With the capture of Gona the Allied left flank was secured, but there were still considerable problems, not the least being that they were operating at the end of a stretched and often unreliable supply system. And the situation at Sanananda, between Gona and Buna, was at a stalemate. Much of the early fighting there had fallen to the 16th Brigade, which had been sorely depleted by its campaigning over the Owen Stanleys. Malaria and battle casualties had cut down its numbers, and although the men's condition was well known to Vasey there was little he could do until he received fresh troops from the 30th Brigade. Indeed, the supply of reinforcements in New Guinea was dwindling. The 2/7th Cavalry Regiment was now retraining as infantry, and the 36th Battalion, another militia unit charged with the defence of Port Moresby, was waiting orders to fly north across the Owen Stanleys.

When the 2/1st AIF Battalion had advanced on Sanananda on November 20, it had come under heavy artillery fire while it was still some kilometres inland. An attempt to outflank the Japanese positions failed, although the Australians got to within metres of the enemy bunkers. The brigade was then forced to dig in while a fresher American 126th Regiment established a roadblock about 1,500 metres behind the main Japanese position. Here about 250 Americans, although virtually surrounded by the enemy, dug in and prevented the Japanese bringing forward supplies or reinforcements. The roadblock had created a weakness behind the two main Japanese positions, but because of the enemy's strength in the area there was some doubt whether the roadblock should be held. Vasey decided that to withdraw the Americans would be a retrograde step and a boost to Japanese morale.

Some Australian artillery — a mere four guns — was flown into the airstrip at Popondetta on November 25, but not even this added firepower could help end the deadlock. At Sanananda, as at Gona, the Australians faced a numerically stronger enemy, dug in, well-prepared and determined to fight.

By the beginning of December the 16th Brigade was utterly exhausted and could do nothing more than hang on in their positions. Realising that this fine formation was spent, Vasey ordered its relief by the militia 30th Brigade which had only two battalions, the 49th and the 55th/53rd. The third battalion, the 39th, was fighting at Gona. In the 16th Brigade, which had lost 209 killed, 400 wounded, 978 evacuated sick and was down to about 800 men, of whom virtually all were infected with malaria and dysentery, there was initial jubilation at the news that they were going to be relieved. But their joy turned to disappointment when the soldiers learned that they would have to hold onto their positions while the understrength militia brigade attacked.

The 30th Brigade was to assault the Sanananda positions from the front in an

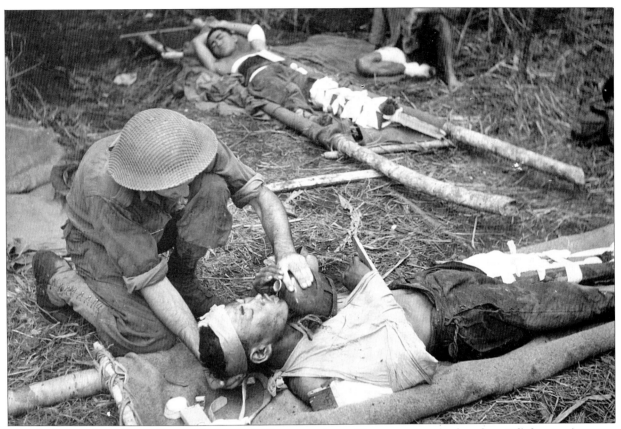

At Gona an Australian soldier cares for a wounded Japanese prisoner. The enemy was seriously under-supplied; a starving Japanese soldier's diary despaired: "There is nothing to eat. Everybody is in a weak and staggering state."

attempt to link up with the Americans at their roadblock. The 55th/53rd Battalion would go in on the left; the 49th on the right, moving up between the positions held by the exhausted 2/1st Battalion. Neither had been in action before, although both contained many veterans of the AIF. The 55th/53rd consisted of the survivors of the old 53rd Battalion which had been sent out of action at Kokoda. Lieutenant Colonel O.A. Kessels, commanding the 49th, issued his orders for the attack late on the night of December 6. Kessels, a militia officer, had not been in action before, his company commanders did not have sufficient time for a reconnaissance of the ground over which they were to attack, nor time to talk to their troops. But each of the rifle companies was about 100 strong, and each man was carrying five days' rations, two grenades, 100 rounds of ammunition and a groundsheet. After spending a miserable night in the rain, the men of the 49th stood-to at 5 am. They watched the artillery and mortars firing before the attack and crossed the start-line promptly at 9.45 am. A sergeant from the exhausted 2/1st, waiting for the militia boys to take over the fight, said thankfully to Sergeant Keith Bretherton of the 49th: "If I had a bag of gold, I'd give you each a handful." One of the 49ers replied, "We don't want gold, we want ammunition."

Within minutes they were taking casualties from their own artillery and mortar fire. In the thick jungle the infantry's radio sets would not work; the only communications were by runner. Because of poor visibility and the lack of communications, the mortar-men had no idea that their bombs were falling short. Then, to add to the 49th's problems, the Japanese began to fire, but the Australians kept going, briefly breaking through the Japanese defences.

Casualties among the officers caused immense problems for the inexperienced troops of the 49th. Within minutes one company lost its commander, its second-in-command and one of its platoon commanders. Not surprisingly it lost direction and momentum. By noon, 60 casualties had passed through the battalion's regimental aid post; by the end of the day the

Swarming with flies in the heat, Japanese dead lie in the shambles of their post at Gona. Of about 18,000 Japanese troops who pulled back to defend the Buna-Gona sector, more than 12,000 died.

battalion had lost 14 officers and 215 men killed or wounded, nearly 60 per cent of its offensive force. The attack was a failure, recalled Warrant Officer Fred Cranston. "It did not dislodge the Japanese from their positions and all the ground that was won was eventually forfeited."

Its sister militia battalion fared even worse. That afternoon, the 55th/53rd attacked on the left hand side of the track, but for a gain of only about 100 metres it lost 130 men, including 28 non-commissioned officers. Many of the NCOs were killed or wounded trying to encourage the men forward. The battalion diarist noted acerbically: "The officers had great difficulty in moving troops forward whilst dense undergrowth made maintenance of control and direction difficult. Troops were prone to go to ground and thus prevented themselves being extricated by fire and movement."

In the roadblock, the Americans were only just hanging on. The Japanese had attacked frequently from different angles, some coming close enough to the American slit trenches to be grabbed by the ankles and pulled in — two Japanese officers had been killed in this hand-to-hand combat. The troops in the roadblock itself remained incapable of taking any offensive action against the Japanese, and resupplying the besieged Americans posed immense difficulties as each party had to fight its way in and then fight its way out again.

Between December 10 and December 15, the Australians received reinforcements from the 36th Battalion and the 2/7th Cavalry Regiment — hopefully they might now force the fight. The 36th Battalion was to relieve the 49th's forward position and attack towards the American roadblock while the 49th was to attempt to cut the Japanese lines of communication. These attacks proved fruitless. Over the next few days, the 2/7th Cavalry attacked several times, each without much success. It lost its commanding officer, who was just one of 80 casualties suffered in the six days before Christmas Eve. The cavalry managed to establish another roadblock, but no real gains were made in dislodging the stubborn Japanese defenders. Sanananda

remained at a stalemate.

Meanwhile, Allied attention was turning towards the joint Australian-American attack at Buna. The American 32nd Division, despite being reinforced by its 127th Regiment, was still making little headway. Blamey wanted to land a strong force of infantry from the sea supported by tanks, but the navy refused to cooperate, unwilling to risk its ships on a coastline littered with uncharted reefs and endangered by marauding enemy aircraft. An angry Blamey wrote to Herring on December 8: "The navy principle is now 'Safety First'. Can you imagine Nelson's reaction to a navy that fears to go where the enemy goes regularly?"

Eventually the navy relented and offered Blamey three corvettes to bring troops from Milne Bay. Blamey had summoned Brigadier George Wootten, commanding the 18th Brigade at Milne Bay, to Port Moresby on December 8. Now, with the three corvettes and a Dutch freighter available, Wootten was ordered to bring two of his battalions and eight American M3 light tanks from the 2/6th Armoured Regiment, and clear the Japanese from the area enclosed by Cape Endaiadere, New Strip, Old Strip and Buna Government Station. To do so, Wootten had to take over from the Americans, and he assumed command of the coastal sector on December 17. The following day, the Queenslanders of the 2/9th Battalion, supported by seven tanks, were ordered to capture the area between the coast and the airstrips. For this Wootten had the support of eight 25-pound guns, three 3.7-inch Howitzers, and one American 105 mm gun. It was a tense night before the attack, the men sleeping only in short spells. The veterans of the 2/9th knew that the Americans had attacked and been thrown back. This, thought Corporal Frank Rolleston, a Bren gunner in the 2/9th Battalion and a veteran of Tobruk and Milne Bay, was an ominous sign. Not only would the Japanese be confident, but they would have rectified any gaps in their defence. "We were told to press our attack home without going to ground or trying to get wounded mates out. In so many words, we 69 were told, 'You are not to stop for anything, so either you get into the Japanese defence line or die trying to get there, as there is definitely no turning back once you go forward.' "

Although the Japanese positions had been so heavily pounded that the vegetation was stripped from the tops of trees, the pillboxes and bunker systems were so well camouflaged that they were still not visible. The men of the 2/9th watched the tanks take up their position in front of them. Near to Rolleston, a 3-inch mortar crew was "putting over bombs as fast as they could drop them down the barrel. I heard later," Rolleston said, "they reckoned they were firing at 16 bombs a minute." The bombs were dropping only 300 to 400 metres ahead.

Suddenly the artillery and mortar fire stopped and the tank in front of Rolleston began to move. "Now off we go," said Corporal Frank Dalton, Rolleston's section commander. The Japanese were waiting.

Almost at once a great storm of fire swept at the Australians from the enemy positions. "The air became alive with the hiss of bullets," said Rolleston. Dalton was hit in the groin, but his section kept going as they had been ordered.

Rolleston passed one of the ill-fated Bren-gun carriers which had been used in the unsuccessful attack two weeks before. As he did, he tripped over the body of one of the crew. It was, said the corporal, "not a pretty sight". Now, beside him, two of his mates were killed. Rolleston kept going, heading for a pillbox to his front. "Almost before I realised it I found myself right in front of the opening of the pillbox. I went down to fire and all I heard was a dull click from the gun — the magazine had been knocked off when I fell over that dead man." Rolleston could not find his number two, Private Russell "Rusty" Bayne, whom he had not seen since the attack began. Like so many of the men close to Rolleston, Bayne had been killed right at the beginning of the attack.

In sheer desperation, Rolleston grabbed another magazine out of his pouch, put it on the Bren and fired a burst into the pillbox. As he did

a Japanese hand came out and threw one hand

Australian 18th Brigade reinforcements for the final assault on Buna crowd an

R.A.N. corvette heading for the beachhead. Three Australian corvettes ferried eight tanks and 2,000 troops through dangerous waters from Milne Bay.

Oblivious to the AIF photographer George Silk, an Australian soldier picks off three Japanese in a pillbox while his mate concentrates on a tree sniper during the bitter fighting at Buna in December 1942.

grenade, then a second. As the last one burst, Rolleston's right-hand man, Lance Corporal Charlie Alder, fired his Tommy gun into the pillbox before he, too, was hit.

The scene of the battle echoed with the continual cry of "Stretcher-bearer, stretcher-bearer", but despite the mounting casualties the men of the 2/9th were pushing forward.

The tanks turned the battle. Moving ahead of the infantry, the tanks were firing their 37 mm guns into the enemy strong-points and pill-boxes. Two companies of the 2/9th advancing with the tanks reached Cape Endaiadere within an hour, then swung right. On the left, however, "C" Company was stopped early,

losing more than half its men before it had covered 100 metres. That afternoon, three tanks arrived in the company position and the infantry were able to move forward again.

Warrant Officer Jim Jesse indicated the company's objectives, the Japanese bunkers, to the tank crews by firing Very lights from a sig-nalling pistol. High explosive rounds from the tanks set the grass on fire; soon some of the bunkers had also caught alight and the defen-ders fled, only to be shot down by the advancing Australians. Other bunkers were ignited with a tin of petrol and a hand grenade. The tanks now forced the fight, but one was knocked out when it bellied on a concealed log and came to a halt.

An Australian machine-gun crew sprays deadly fire into a Japanese pillbox in the coconut groves near Buna. Corporal Charles Knight (left) was shot dead shortly before this photograph was taken.

Japanese riflemen swarmed over it, firing into the observation slits, and trying to set it on fire. Another tank was burned when a magnetic bomb exploded against it. By nightfall the Australians were on the Japanese reserve line. The 2/9th, at the cost of 171 officers and men, had broken through the forward defences.

General Eichelberger was pleased with the results. "It was a spectacular and dramatic assault, and a brave one," he said. "From the New Strip to the sea was about half a mile. American troops wheeled to the west in support, and other Americans were assigned to mopping-up duties. But behind the tanks went the fresh and jaunty Aussies, tall, moustached, erect, with their blazing Tommy guns winging before them. Concealed Japanese positions, which were even more formidable than our patrols had indicated, burst into flame. There was the greasy smell of tracer fire and heavy machine-gun fire from barricades and entrenchments. Steadily tanks and infantrymen advanced through the spare, high coconut trees, seemingly impervious to the heavy opposition."

Herring wrote to Blamey that the tanks and the 2/9th had fought magnificently. "The outstanding factors so far are three. The first is Wootten's leadership, the second is the value of the tanks for which we have to thank you, and the third the capacity of seasoned AIF troops."

In the Buna coconut plantation, smoke pours from a shattered enemy pillbox (left) blasted by an Australian-manned Stuart tank while infantrymen snipe

at fleeing Japanese. The soldier standing behind the tank was killed seconds later.

During the drive towards Giropa Point, an infantry officer warns an Australian tank crew of an enemy pillbox to the right. After tanks breached the Japanese strongholds, infantry rushed in with grenades and ammonal charges.

The next day the 2/9th attacked again, this time after the positions ahead had been pounded by American bombers. By the end of the day, the battalion was on the line of Simemi Creek and here they stopped while a crossing point for the tanks was found. A patrol from the South Australian 2/10th Battalion, after wading through swamps up to their necks, found a suitable crossing on December 22. Now the 2/9th attacked once more, this time to take the strip of land between the creek and the sea. Casualties had forced the battalion commander, Lieutenant Colonel C.J. Cummings, to form a composite company, so he had only three rifle companies to use. At first, the attack went well, but then a machine-gun opened fire on "A" Company from the left. As the advance halted for this machine-gun to be taken out, a Japanese anti-aircraft gun, turned around and used in a ground role, began firing into the battalion headquarters grouped near the start-line.

In Sergeant Rolleston's company, the commander, Captain Roger Griffin, sent for a tank to knock out the machine-gun causing so much trouble. The tank made its way forward across the boggy ground but missed the Australians and kept going. Griffin lost his temper when he saw the tank pass the enemy post, and he began screaming at it at the top of his voice. He then raced forward, knocking on the side of the tank to attract its attention. But, in the heat of the moment, he was killed. So heavy had casualties been that day, now Griffin's company was commanded by a sergeant, Steve McCready, while the composite company was commanded by the redoubtable Warrant Officer Jesse. The heavy fighting continued and at the end of the day, the 2/9th Battalion had lost another eight officers and 50 men. But the remainder of the battalion were dug in.

In six days the first phase of Wootten's attack had been completed. Now Wootten ordered for-

76

On the wet sand of Buna beach, Japanese corpses roll in the tide near half-sunk and grounded troop barges. Hundreds of American 127th Regiment GIs also littered this beach after heavy fighting in December 1942.

ward the South Australians of the 2/10th. They attacked on Christmas Eve westward along the Old Strip, with the remaining four tanks. The infantry and tanks moved forward for half an hour before they were engaged by a Japanese anti-aircraft gun. Within minutes, all four Australian tanks, 50 metres apart, had been hit and knocked out. The attack faltered.

On Christmas Day and Boxing Day, the 2/10th tried again; now the companies were reduced to about one third their strength. The Japanese, emboldened by their successes, were counter-attacking with greater ferocity. Wootten brought up the 2/12th Battalion, which had been detached on Goodenough Island, and he threw it into the attack with more tanks. They went towards the coast, clearing away enemy troops between the Simemi River mouth and Giropa Point. Finally on New Year's Day, 1943, the stubborn Japanese defenders at Buna were defeated, although mopping up — never

easy against such a ferocious enemy — continued for days. In 16 days the 18th Brigade had lost 55 officers and 808 men, including 22 officers and 284 other ranks killed. The Japanese dead were put at 1,390.

The Americans lost 1,900 dead and wounded during this action as they fought their way into Buna mission. They had been reinforced by two fresh battalions of the 127th Regiment, but even so it had taken them until January 2 to capture the mission and link up with the Australians at Giropa Point.

The Papuan campaign had seen for the first time the Americans and Australians under General MacArthur fighting side by side. The beachhead battles, however, would be the last time they would join together in such large numbers. Now, with Buna won, their attention shifted to the stalemate at Sanananda, where fighting had been quiet during the last two weeks of December.

American soldiers of 163rd Regiment open fire into a dug-out at Sanananda to kill a Japanese sniper who ambushed Australian ammunition-carriers.

At least 1,600 Japanese were buried at Sanananda and 2,000 were evacuated by barge before the village fell on January 18, 1943.

After Gona's capture, the Australian militiamen of the 39th Battalion were sent on to Sanananda, where they joined the roadblock garrison. Now the battered 18th Brigade, with its all-important tanks and artillery, was ordered to this front as well. Also, Americans of the 41st Division began to replace Ivan Dougherty's weary Australians of the 21st Brigade.

The 18th Brigade began to attack on January 12, but the country was unsuitable for tanks, and the Allies ran up against the pillbox and bunker defence which had stalled them at Buna. Vasey became depressed; it was all too reminiscent of the tactics he had cut his teeth on in the First World War in France and Flanders. To break the deadlock he decided to force out the defenders with a concerted artillery and mortar offensive. Meanwhile, in the difficult swamps, jungle and kunai grass the 18th Brigade kept at their tasks for another week, patrolling aggressively against the staunch Japanese, whose main defences were positioned north of the Sanananda road.

American troops were also in the thick of it, attacking north out of their roadblock as well as mopping up isolated enemy pockets to its south. And, another U.S. force was heading west out of Buna to clean out the Japanese still occupying positions along the coast. The Allies kept bashing away at the enemy, advancing yard by painful yard until finally the resistance gave way and Sanananda fell on January 21, 1943. The fight took 800 American battle casualties and 2,700 Australians.

The Papuan campaign was over, six months to the day after it had begun. It had been costly for both sides. The 39th Battalion, who had seen action during practically the entire period, was typically depleted. Now it left Sanananda after a month of fighting there — with just seven officers and 25 other ranks. There were no vehicles for fit soldiers on the 20-kilometre journey back to Dobodura airfield; that luxury was only for the stragglers who fell out during the debilitating trek. Their proud commanding officer, Lieutenant Colonel Honner, marched the exhausted men with parade ground precision. They were "haggard, silent, sweating scarecrows under the tropic sun," Honner wrote. "And when an amazed bystander enquired, 'What mob's this?' we kept our eyes straight ahead — all except my second-in-command at the end of the line, who barked, 'This is not a mob,' and added, relenting, 'This is the 39th!' "

The Japanese were similarly staunch in the face of adversity. They, too, were exhausted from the earlier mountain fighting. Holed up on the coastline since November, they were stricken by hunger and disease, and they had received few supplies or reinforcements — Allied air attacks often helped by coastwatchers had virtually annihilated enemy convoys from their main base at Rabaul, and small naval units operating close to shore had also limited enemy movements up and down the coast.

But, Japanese Imperial Headquarters in Tokyo were not yet ready to give up their hold on New Guinea. Early in January, after a lack of progress in the Solomons, local Japanese commanders had been ordered to abandon aggressive moves on Guadalcanal and to concentrate their efforts in New Guinea by moving their beachhead troops north to Lae and Salamaua. And so, during the height of the final Allied push on Sanananda, Japan's 18th Army commander Lieutenant General Hatazo Adachi told his troops there to prepare to evacuate the coast. In the last week of the Sanananda battle, more than 1,000 sick and wounded were taken out, while a similar number managed to slip through Allied lines and escape to the west of Gona. They left close to 2,000 dead in the area.

Despite such losses, both of manpower and territory, the enemy hung on tenaciously to their plans to control Papua and New Guinea and, specifically, Port Moresby. Although they had given up their bases on the northeast coast of Papua, Japanese forces now looked at a new route to their objectives. The fighting moved north to the mandated territory of New Guinea, and it was to prove as ferocious as ever.

A vivid Japanese propaganda leaflet air-dropped on Allied troops reminds soldiers of their erotic desires and fear of death.

In a Hollywood-style romance scene on a Japanese warfare leaflet, a soldier embraces his girlfriend beneath a full moon. When the leaflet is opened, the lower legs of the young male lover become the grotesquely twisted legs of a battlefield corpse, transforming the love scene into one of violent death. Flip-up cards, showing the unpleasant alternatives for those who did not surrender, were a favourite propaganda technique.

EXPLOITING FEAR AND DOUBT

Until their invasion of China in 1931, Japan's militarists regarded propaganda, or "thought war" as they termed it, as a Western deceit unworthy of the true spirit of Japanese warrior-hood. They soon learned quickly from the West, where Nazi Germany in the 1930s had demon-strated the power of slogans, poster art, radio broadcasts and films to indoctrinate the masses. Japan's senior commanders adapted these forms to bend the will of their nation and later the conquered peoples of Asia. As well, the psychological warfare techniques of the British and Germans in World War I became a model for Japan's Pacific campaign.

Using powerful short-wave radio transmitters based in Batavia, Saigon and Singapore, the Japanese beamed daily English language broad-casts to audiences in Australia and America, and to Allied troops in the islands. One trick was to have Allied prisoners of war send messages to their families during the broadcast — anxious relatives would listen to the entire propaganda "news" program.

The Japanese employed a young Japanese-American girl to do daily 15-minute broadcasts for American troops. She became famous as the huskily voiced "Tokyo Rose", talking sexily, playing popular music, and exploiting the GIs' homesickness with sentimental descriptions of an America they might not live to see.

The Japanese also air-dropped thousands of lurid propaganda leaflets on enemy troops, aimed primarily at creating divisions amongst Allied soldiers of different nationalities. America was accused of intending to make Australia a state of the U.S., and of sacrificing Australian lives for its own gains. Pornographic leaflets showed Australian girls in the sexual embraces of drunken and lecherous GIs while their boyfriends and husbands fought in the jungle. And Australian and New Zealand soldiers were told that they were fighting Britain's battles for her; while Anzac troops died on distant shores most of the British Army stayed home.

On the Allied side, the Far Eastern Liaison Office (FELO) conducted a similar radio and paper war on a grand scale against the Japanese. As Japan's military fortunes worsened, half starved and desperate enemy soldiers gave themselves up, often in response to leaflet drops or "surrender" speeches over megaphones.

Despite the enormous effort expended on it the psychological warfare campaign by both sides lacked credibility as an effective weapon. The doubts and fears that Japanese propaganda addressed may have been present to varying extents in the minds of Aussie soldiers, but the war of thoughts left few casualties. Hunger, homesickness, fear of death, sexual frustration and loneliness were real enough for most soldiers. And for some Australians so too were resentments and suspicions about the Yanks. Corporal Clifford Yates of the 2/9th Battalion expressed a common Australian attitude: "The Americans were over-paid, over-fed, over-equipped and over-dressed; thank God, though they were over here." But the strenuous and often sophisticated efforts of the Japanese propagandists to manipulate fears, cravings and jealousies failed. The Diggers' bonds to their nation, families and fellow soldiers were too strong to be challenged. And there was always the greatest fear of all — Japanese victory.

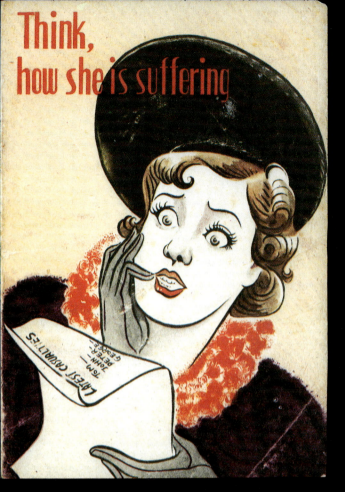

Think, how she is suffering

On the cover of a Japanese leaflet, a grieving wife sees her husband's name on the casualty list. But, when opened, the leaflet reveals the Australian soldier waving a white flag of surrender and walking away, wounded but alive, from a horrific corpse-strewn battlefield. The image of wife or girlfriend begging for her man's return was often used — a strange contradiction to accusations of Australian female infidelity.

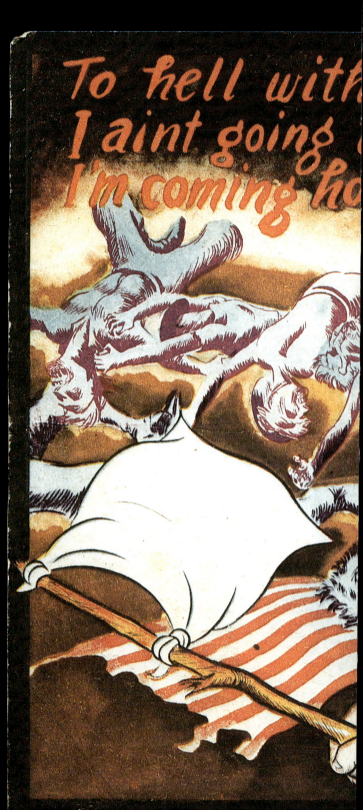

To hell with
I aint going
I'm coming ho

An anti-Yank leaflet sows doubts in the Australian soldier's mind. While the Digger in New Guinea fights a desperate battle in toeless boots and tattered uniform, the glamorous Yank back home steals his girl.

An imperialist U.S. President Roosevelt annexes Australia while its troops drown in the bow wave of Japan's unstoppable navy. Japanese propaganda hammered the theme that Australia was being used as an American and British puppet.

In a pornographic leaflet designed to arouse suspicion and jealousy, a Digger faced with a grisly and futile death is haunted

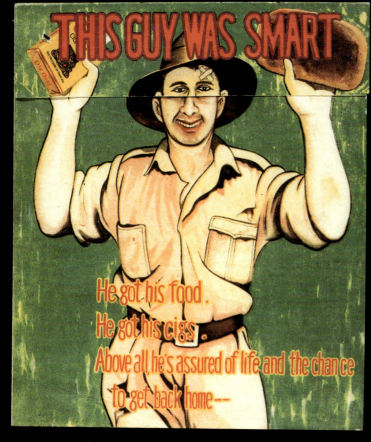

THIS GUY WAS SMART

He got his food.

He got his cigs.

Above all he's assured of life and the chance

to get back home--

Left: A flip-up card shows how a wounded, hungry Australian soldier would receive food, cigarettes and medical aid if (right) he simply raised his hands in surrender. The Allied propagandists made identical promises to Japanese troops.

Iron-rationed Stranded.
Nothing but dog biscuits
   Day after day, positively.
   How about a dish of salad like this?
   For a change of diet.. just a change of mind.

A Japanese propaganda card appeals to an Allied soldier's appetite "to change his mind". For the Japanese, whose starving troops in New Guinea resorted to cannibalism to survive, hunger seemed a powerful motive for surrender.

BY DOING THIS
He got his food .
He got his cigs .
Above all, he's assured of life and the chan ce
to get back home--

3

GAINING GROUND
IN NEW GUINEA

Australian troops narrowly saved the vital Wau airstrip from enemy capture after a brave, last-ditch stand bought time for airborne reinforcements. Then, fighting bitterly for every ridge, the Japanese were forced to defend ferociously around Salamaua.

With the reverses of Japan's forces in the Owen Stanleys and at Milne Bay, and its defenders gone from the northeastern Papuan coast, the bases at Lae and Salamaua and further to the north, Madang and Wewak, became increasingly important to both the Japanese and the Allies. Lae and Salamaua were extremely vital because from there the Japanese could dominate both the Dampier Strait and the Vitiaz Strait between New Guinea and New Britain, thus preventing any Allied advance along the northern New Guinea coast. As well, those two port townships under the Huon Peninsula were essential in Japan's continuing plan to advance over the mountains and take Port Moresby.

They had landed at Lae and Salamaua in March 1942. At that time the only Australian soldiers in the area were among four platoons of the New Guinea Volunteer Rifles, and after a short skirmish the NGVR troops withdrew, leaving both towns to the enemy. From headquarters at Wau, the Allied soldiers patrolled close to Japanese positions along the coastline, making nuisance raids, and collecting valuable intelligence, but this however was the limit of

Ray Ewer's eye-patched bronze bust "Walking Wounded" graphically expresses the agony of an Australian battle victim.

their capacities. They were too few in number and too lightly equipped to be any serious threat to the Japanese garrisons.

The NGVR platoons were later reinforced with the well-trained and highly individualistic commandos of Australia's independent companies. Under the command of Lieutenant Colonel N.L. Fleay, "Kanga Force", as it was called, kept up a vigorous regime of patrolling, and it succeeded in bluffing the Japanese, preventing them from taking Wau for the remainder of 1942. And Japanese commanders were kept so diverted by Kanga Force that they did not switch reinforcements to the fighting in the Owen Stanleys and around Buna, Gona and Sanananda.

At about the time the Japanese decided to withdraw from Sanananda, they also took the decision to reinforce Lae and Salamaua. The 102nd Infantry Regimental Group left Rabaul in an escorted convoy made up of 10 destroyers and transports, but the convoy's movements were detected by Allied coastwatchers, by the build-up of Japanese shipping in Rabaul Harbour, and from decoded interceptions of Japanese naval radio traffic. Allied aircraft, including Hudson bombers from the RAAF's Numbers 2 and 13 Squadrons, as well as Beaufighters, were sent from bases in northern Australia to intercept the convoy and sink the ships. In the ensuing battle, two Japanese ships were known to have gone to the bottom, and about 50 of their covering aircraft were shot down, but the majority of the Japanese regiment landed in Lae on January 7. Allied losses were 10 aircraft.

Blamey had been prepared for the Japanese moves. On January 8 he wrote to General Herring, commanding New Guinea Force: "Whether the intention of this force is to push forward from Lae and Salamaua towards Wau remains to be seen. This event has always been present in my mind and I have kept the 17th Brigade AIF intact either to meet this threat or as the spearhead of an advance in this area."

The Japanese intentions quickly became clear; their orders were to advance on and capture Wau and its well-developed airfield. Once again, the land objectives for the armies were airfields. Salamaua was to be the base for this Japanese offensive, and by January 16 they had concentrated a striking force there, ready for an advance first south to the village of Mubo and then southwest to Wau.

To counter this offensive, Blamey and Herring had the battle-toughened 17th Brigade assembled at Milne Bay, but by the time its men left for Wau it was drastically understrength, largely because of malaria. The soldiers had been put to work at Milne Bay shovelling gravel to make roads in the swamps, and the appalling conditions and climate had taken their toll. In the 2/6th Battalion, 113 men had been evacuated from Milne Bay in November suffering from malaria.

On January 8, 1943, Brigadier M.J. Moten, commanding the 17th Brigade, was ordered by Blamey to take over Kanga Force then based at Wau, but bad weather and the closure of Wau airfield delayed the early arrival of most of the 17th Brigade; it was January 19 before the 2/6th was complete on the ground. During this vital build-up phase, in a race against time and the Japanese, the 2/6th's companies were spread much wider than a prudent battalion commander would have liked. But because of the weather, there was simply no choice; the battalion had to do some of the tasks which would eventually be given to the entire brigade.

For the Australians, the Wau airfield was vital ground. Holding it was essential. The first of the 2/6th to arrive, "B" and "D" companies, were each allocated areas well away from Wau. "D" Company, under the command of Captain Bill Dexter, was sent to Timne, 45 kilometres north down the Bulolo Valley where it was to watch for any Japanese movement from Lae towards Wau. "B" Company, under Major Jo Jones, had linked up with the commandos — the "beards and bullshit brigade" as they were dubbed by the orthodox infantry soldiers — and were covering the approaches from Wau through the village of Mubo.

"A" Company, under Captain Bill Sherlock,

was ordered along the Buisaval Track to Ballam's village where it had to patrol the Wandumi area and the eastern entrance to the Wau valley. "HQ" Company and "C" Company were entrusted with the vital defence of the Wau airfield itself. The 2/6th commander, Lieutenant Colonel F.G. Wood, had also been warned of the need to move to Bulolo once the rest of the brigade arrived at Wau. And so, soon after his arrival he set off to Bulolo on a reconnaissance — his company commanders had their own responsibilities.

Major Jones's company was the first to discover that, at the same time as the battalion was deploying on the approaches to Wau, the Japanese were moving to capture the airfield there; Jones had contacted the commando force operating in the area and was told that the Japanese were closing in north from Mubo. The commander of the independent company, Major T.F.B. MacAdie, was worried that the Japanese might have found a new track towards the Black Cat mine from the east. Thus, on

January 20, Jones set out with a young commando officer, Lieutenant Pat Dunshea, and a patrol to attempt to get behind the Japanese at Mubo. Jones later recalled: "We counted some 60 Japanese on the horizon moving towards Wau. We also stumbled on one of their camps."

His information was quickly passed back, but was not received with any great alarm at Moten's headquarters. Five days later, another patrol produced more evidence that the Japanese were moving in strength along a track towards Wau which was known to the old New Guinea hands in the NGVR but had been overlooked by Moten in planning his defences. Again the Japanese intentions were not grasped. Moten believed that the Japanese force was not much more than a strong raiding party, perhaps 300 men at most. In fact, the enemy had nearly 3,000 members of the 102nd Infantry Regimental Group on their final approach to the assembly area for the coming attack on Wau.

The 2/6th Battalion was ordered to bring back the troops it had previously sent ahead to Bulolo; now it was to raid the Japanese "patrol" simultaneously from three directions. Its attack was to go in on the morning of January 28. But the Japanese struck first, 2,000 of them blitzing Captain Sherlock's company of about 100 men occupying a bare ridge near Wandumi. The surprised Australians had no shovels or picks to dig trenches from which to fight; they used their hands and their mess tins.

All through that morning and into the afternoon the Japanese attacked repeatedly, supported by fire from heavy machine-guns and mortars. Grimly, Sherlock's men hung on. At 3.10 pm, the battalion's log reported: "Things very hot. Any help now may be too late. One platoon overrun. Am counter-attacking now."

The Australians hit back. Half an hour later the battalion log recorded: "More ammunition needed. Recaptured original position with counter-attack. Little ammunition left. Japs weakening. Good chance of holding but can not guarantee." There were now only 20 Australians left. Back in Moten's headquarters,

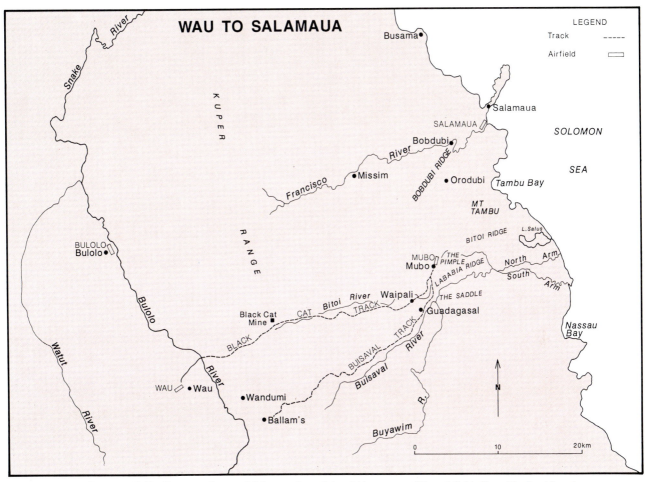

WAU TO SALAMAUA

In January 1943 a Japanese force at Mubo struck south in a bid to capture Wau airfield. But, ridge by ridge, the Australians rolled back enemy positions to the coast, finally taking Salamaua in September.

the Kanga Force commander had reacted slowly to Sherlock's original reports of the Japanese attack in strength at Wandumi. Late in the afternoon, when he realised the gravity of Sherlock's position, he ordered Major J.W. Duffy's company of the 2/7th Battalion forward to help the hard-pressed captain. There was now no reserve force left in Wau. Moten signalled Herring in Port Moresby: "You must expedite arrival troops this area."

Duffy's men had only just landed at Wau, and they immediately set off on a four-hour march to Wandumi. But not even these extra troops could make a difference. The Japanese were in such strength that it was easy for them to bypass the small force of Australians. Under the pressure of the continued attacks, some of the Australians in Sherlock's company tried to pull back prematurely. A member of 9 Platoon, "A" Company, Private Bill Hooper came down the

hill from his forward position towards Sherlock's headquarters. "We had just reached the bottom of the hill when Captain Sherlock came hurtling towards us, grabbed a rifle and bayonet, and led us back up the hill," Hooper recalled. "We were only 13 strong at that stage. It was only due to his leading us that we went back up that hill again. He led the whole way. I saw him kill four Japanese with the bayonet. So we reached the top of the hill."

Finally Sherlock decided to pull back in the early hours of January 29. In the dark, and with the Japanese pressing all around, withdrawal was an extremely difficult task. Sherlock, ever the conscientious leader, knew his personal responsibility was to be the last man out. "We got down to the creek," said Hooper. "Captain Sherlock and several of the troops crossed it by the log bridge. He was heard to call out amid all the noise of yelling and firing, 'Are you Japanese

93

or Australians?' and a few seconds later, 'I'll give you Japanese you bastards.' There was a burst of fire, then silence.''

Sherlock was killed at once. For his brave action, he was mentioned in despatches. Most members of the 2/6th believed he should have been given the Victoria Cross. His efforts especially, and those of his men at Wandumi, had saved Wau.

As well as the strong force which was held up by Sherlock's valiant company, the Japanese were approaching Wau from other directions. A transport driver told Moten at 7 pm on January 28 that he had seen a body of Japanese troops marching towards Wau about five kilometres southeast of the airstrip. Moten ordered Lieutenant Colonel Danny Starr of the 2/5th Battalion to bring back his two companies from Ballam's to Wau. It was a hell of a trip. The men left about dark and marched all night in the pouring rain down the track towards Wau. They made it over the swing bridge at the Bulolo River about 4 am and there joined the man-made road into the town itself. The soldiers were tiring, trudging in platoons and sections along on each side of the road. One company's second-in-command, Captain Tex Brown, re-ported to his superior, Captain Cam Bennett, that the men were exhausted and too tired to go on. But Bennett walked along the column, urging them on with threats and jokes. Then, in the fading dark less than two kilometres from Wau airfield, the men of Bennett's company saw a large group of figures sitting back from both sides of the road.

''Who the Christ are they?'' one Digger asked.

''Bloody natives, probably too scared to come into town,'' Bennett replied.

In fact, the figures were two battalions of Japanese infantry, waiting for their attack on Wau. Bennett's company had almost passed through them, but when the Japanese realised who the Australians were, the Japanese opened fire from about 600 metres. ''It had exactly the right effect'', Bennett recalled laconically. ''We almost ran, exhausted though we were, into the 'drome area.''

There they were allotted an area, the east side of the strip, and dug in. All day Allied planes landed, bringing the remainder of the 2/5th Battalion, followed by the 2/7th. That night the enemy attacked the airfield in strength.

The first thrust fell on a position held by Major K.R. Walker's company of the 2/7th Battalion. Walker's headquarters was pushed back. In the confusion of the fighting, he organised a quick counter-attack party and was about to launch an assault when he realised his objective was held by soldiers from the 2/5th Battalion. The Australians' hastily prepared positions held, and the following morning Moten's force received a handy boost in the form of a section of two guns from the 2/1st Field Regiment. The guns had landed at 9.15 am; little more than two hours later they had their positions established and were firing rounds in support of the defenders.

On the afternoon of January 31, the men of the 2/7th began a counter-attack that was aimed to push the Japanese back from the approaches to Wau airfield. At first, the troops made only slow progress up a slippery, muddy slope against an enemy with well-hidden machine-gun positions and snipers in the trees. One company, temporarily halted by a machine-gun, watched with amazement as 400 Japanese appeared, coming towards them along a road from the southeast. The Australians waited until the Japanese were about 200 metres away, and then opened fire with their rifles and machine-guns. At the same time, the two 25-pounders added their fire. The gun commander wrote later, ''The Japs advanced in column along the road right in front of me — and I had a field day with them.''

A few minutes later, RAAF Beaufighters swept over the Japanese positions, adding their machine-gun fire to the melee. The Beaufighters, known to the troops as ''Whispering Death'' because of their gentle engine noises, fired 22,000 rounds of cannon and machine-gun fire in support of the ground troops. Some of the fire was directed by army officers flying with the RAAF, and some

Springing straight into action to defend the strategic aerodrome at Wau, 17th Brigade soldiers leap from their transport plane. On January 30, 1943, troops flown in by 60 planes were deployed to block the encircling Japanese force.

coordinated by RAAF officers working on the ground with the troops. In the fighting around the Wau airfield, the Beaufighters and the slow-moving Wirraways of No. 4 Squadron were invaluable, the latter even delivering 3-inch mortar tubes and tripods by parachute.

Even in the face of such concentrated firepower, many of the entrenched Japanese held their ground. The 2/7th's counter-attack bogged down when the company moving up the spur was unable to go any further that day. Now, however, more reinforcements were arriving in Douglas DC3 aircraft, which were landing under direct fire from Japanese machine-gunners and snipers. "Right! Where are the bastards? Let's at them!" shouted one soldier as he jumped down from the aircraft waving his sub-machine-gun. As he did, he was shot by a sniper at the other end of the aerodrome. The hapless Digger went back as a casualty in the same aircraft — his battle at Wau had lasted just 30 seconds.

For Moten, the crisis in holding onto Wau

airfield had passed by the morning of January 31. What remained, however, was to push the Japanese back from the surrounding country. In this stage of the fighting, Captain Jo Gullett's company of the 2/6th Battalion was fighting along the Black Cat Trail, which came down from Salamaua. Gullett's commanding officer, Lieutenant Colonel Wood, was a direct man. "Don't muck about," Wood said. "I don't want a lot of skirmishing. Go straight through them. Is that clear?"

The track ran along a ridge. Gullett took the right side with Sergeant Neville Gibbons and most of the 2/6th Battalion men; and the commando officer, Lieutenant J. W. W. Blezard, took the left. Almost at once the force ran into a machine-gun post on Blezard's side. He engaged the machine-gun while Gibbons and Gullett worked up the other side of the track close enough to throw grenades. "Blezard's men charged in and finished them," Gullett said. "We were apparently approaching a Japanese staging camp because we passed many huts and

DOOMED CONVOY

Japan's Army lost heavily in their attack on Wau airfield in late January 1943. The subsequent reverse when Australian forces countered and forced Japanese troops back to their original strike base at Mubo alarmed 8th Area Army commander General Imamura greatly. From his Rabaul headquarters, the Japanese general feared for the safety of his bases at Lae and Salamaua on the Huon Gulf Coast. Both locations had strategically important ports and airfields, allowing the Japanese to dominate the Vitiaz Strait and to block any Allied push north along the New Guinea coast. Imamura decided that Lae had to be reinforced as quickly as possible.

As there was no quick overland route south to Lae from Japan's coastal bases at Madang or Wewak, Imamura took the calculated risk of sending a troop convoy direct from Rabaul to Lae itself. Such a convoy would be so vulnerable to air attack during its passage through the Bismarck Sea and the Vitiaz Strait that senior Japanese commanders estimated its probable losses at 50 per cent. Even so, the plan went ahead, and on February 28, 1943, a convoy of eight transport ships carrying more than 6,000 Japanese troops and marines, escorted by eight destroyers, sailed from Rabaul.

General Kenney's 5th Air Force, which included American and Australian squadrons and aircraft, had anticipated such moves and prepared tactically with bombers and fighters at Dobodura and Moresby airfields. Late in the afternoon on March 1, the Japanese convoy was spotted through cloud cover by an American Liberator bomber. The alarm was raised. The next day a massive dawn bombing raid by six RAAF Bostons on Lae aerodrome discouraged enemy fighters using the base and limited the air cover available for the convoy, which was still out of medium bomber range. At 10 am, however, a force of B-17 heavy bombers (Flying Fortresses) attacked the ships, sinking one destroyer and one transport ship. Two other destroyers picked up about 900 survivors and delivered them safely to their Lae base that night in a fast run under cover of darkness.

The remaining 13 ships were shadowed by an RAAF Catalina as they

A Japanese transport ship is well ablaze after a low-level bombing run. Australian cameraman Damien Parer, aboard a Beaufighter, caught battle highlights on film.

slipped through the Vitiaz Strait that night. They were rejoined by the two fast destroyers from Lae, and by nine the following morning the 15-ship convoy was steaming over a smooth sea 48 kilometres southeast of Cape Cretin at the eastern tip of the Huon Peninsula. The ships were strung out in a loose formation, heading for their destination 150 kilometres away. Above them flew a fighter escort.

Suddenly wave after wave of Allied planes blotted out the sun. From the south, B-17 heavy bombers, B-25 medium bombers (Mitchells) and A-20 light Bombers (Bostons) swooped on the destroyers and transport ships. The bombers made low-level attacks, skipping 500-lb bombs at the waterline close to the ships.

Zeroes dived to attack the bombers and were pounced on by American Lightning fighters. Meanwhile RAAF Beaufighters made daring attacks at masthead height, strafing gun-crews and troops on the ships. The Japanese craft were crowded with troops, and their guns spat back at the marauding Allied aircraft, the destroyers peeling off to meet the attackers from the south. The transports had little chance: within 15 minutes the flagship *Shirayuki* was sunk and the seven remaining transports were listing, ablaze or sunk.

After desperate attempts to pick up survivors during the next two days, only four destroyers of the original eight limped back to Rabaul on March 5 with about 3,800 troops. American torpedo boats and Bostons, Mitchells and Beaufighters swept the Huon Gulf destroying barges and rafts carrying Japanese. Approximately 3,000 Japanese troops, marines and ships' crews were lost. Only the 900 men from the original wave made it to Lae.

The Battle of the Bismarck Sea was a devastating blow to the Japanese Navy and Army. Reinforcement of New Guinea was attempted only in a secretive and piecemeal fashion thereafter, and remained a constant headache for the Japanese. As well, the loss of the transport *Kembu Maru*, which was laden with aviation fuel, destroyed any hope of strengthening Japan's air power in the Lae-Salamaua area.

But most importantly, Japan's military nerve centre at Rabaul was shown to be vulnerable, pinched between two Allied fronts in New Guinea and the Solomons. General MacArthur recognised the importance of the result, later describing the Battle of the Bismarck Sea as ''the decisive aerial engagement of the war in the southwest Pacific.''

there were a lot of sick and dead. At the centre of this camp were two machine-guns supported by infantry. We had trouble getting forward as they were well-sited and concealed. When I reckoned we were close enough I sang out to Blezard above the racket of the firing, telling him that I would throw grenades and we would then rush in.''

Gibbons and Gullett threw the grenades. As they went forward, they could hear Blezard calling on his men. ''There was a crescendo of firing and then silence,'' Gullett recalled. ''The half-dozen Japanese on my side were all dead. One of my men had a nasty face wound. Blezard's runner came across to tell me Blezard had been killed.''

Gullett's force went on like this for about an hour and a half, killing more than 20 Japanese, not counting the sick and wounded who were lying around the camp. ''I did not wish to kill these, but one of them we had left alive fired on us after we passed, and after that the men took no chances with them,'' Gullett said.

After this fighting, Jo Gullett went back to his battalion headquarters position overlooking the Wau valley. Looking down, they could see the Japanese infantry attacking the airfield held by the 2/5th and the 2/7th. The Australians' artillery was firing over open sights at a range of a few hundred metres. Then, in came a force of Allied fighters, boring into the Japanese. ''It was a thrilling sight,'' Gullett recalled. ''Planes wheeling and rolling and smoking under us. In all the war, this might have been the only time when foot soldiers looked down on an air battle.'' In the ensuing fight, the Allies lost one Wirraway and a Douglas transport; the Japanese three bombers and 15 fighters.

As the Japanese pulled back, the Australians kept harassing them. The fighting was vicious. The Australians did not know whether the Japanese were retreating or whether they were simply pulling back to re-form for a second attack on Wau. But, by the end of February 1943, Moten's brigade had cleared the Japanese from around Wau. What was left of the 102nd Regimental Group was back in Mubo. ''It was a

near thing,'' one staff officer, Colonel E. G. Keogh, wrote later. ''If the Japanese had moved about a week earlier they would have probably taken Wau. While that would not have given them Port Moresby, it would have created a very awkward situation for the Allies.''

In the month that followed, Kanga Force held a line between the villages of Guadagasal and Waipali and patrolled vigorously forward to Mubo. The Japanese, however, were not easily deterred, still hoping to capture Wau as a preliminary to making another attempt for Port Moresby via the Markham and Snake River valleys. Reinforcements now sailed from Rabaul, but a large Japanese convoy charged with transporting the vital troops and accompanying supplies and fuel for its New Guinea forces was virtually destroyed in the Bismarck Sea early in March. It was a savage blow to Japan's plans.

With Wau secure, and the Japanese reeling, the Allies focussed on an overall strategic plan to take the enemy's major base in Rabaul. This was at least one Pacific objective that Allied leaders had agreed upon in January 1943 when Winston Churchill and Franklin D. Roosevelt met in Casablanca in North Africa to discuss the future conduct of the war. The Casablanca conference, however, was dominated by strategic thinking in the Mediterranean, with the Pacific war well down the list of priorities. Everyone at Casablanca seemed to accept that Rabaul would be in Allied hands within six months, but such optimistic expectations ran directly counter to the experience of the local commanders in the South Pacific. MacArthur, Admiral Chester Nimitz commanding the U.S. Pacific Fleet, and Admiral F. Halsey, commanding the Allied South Pacific Forces, had found that the Japanese were far too determined to allow for such heroic assumptions about early successes.

Guadalcanal was a case in point. After a series of naval battles in the Solomons in mid-November 1942, fighting on the island had continued to be hard, although the Americans there were not in danger of being ejected. In the

Patrolling in the Wau-Mubo area, 3rd Division troops stay on the alert. Operational reports described jungle patrols as "rain, mud, rottenness, stench, gloom and the constant expectancy of death from behind the impenetrable screen of green."

next month U.S. forces were heavily reinforced, and there was a massive increase in Allied air strength as well, so that early in January 1943 America had double the forces of their enemy on Guadalcanal. The Japanese nevertheless resisted all attacks, but in the last half of January Japanese commanders ordered a withdrawal from Guadalcanal, and the Americans finally claimed victory on the island on February 9. Of more than 35,000 Japanese who had fought there for longer than six months, close to 25,000 had been killed, taken prisoner, or died of disease. It had been a desperate struggle and one which U.S. commanders would not forget easily; they had lost 1,600 men killed and more than 4,000 wounded.

Most of the 13,000 Japanese troops went back to Rabaul, which remained Japan's major base in the region. It was now clear that the Allies could not capture Rabaul in one operation. There were insufficient ships, landing craft, aircraft and other materiel available to the Pacific commanders. As well, it was also clear than the Australian 6th and 7th Divisions, the militia brigades, and the American 32nd and 41st Divisions needed to be rested and reinforced, as did the U.S. marines following their long and exhausting struggle on Guadalcanal. After much preparation, planning and counter-planning, the Chiefs of Staff issued on March 28, 1943, a directive which effectively cancelled their order of the previous July to capture Rabaul. Now the objectives were to be more modest: the seizure of Woodlark and Kiriwina islands to allow the construction of airfields; the capture of Salamaua, Lae, Finschhafen and Madang in New Guinea; the occupation of western New Britain; and the occupation of the Solomon Islands as far north as southern Bougainville.

MacArthur regrouped his forces for these offensives: they became "Alamo Force" under the command of the American Lieutenant General Walter Krueger, and the 54,000-strong New Guinea Force under the command of the

After fighting to the coast, a 2/6th Battalion patrol links up with an American landing force at Nassau Bay on June 30, 1943. The American beachhead reinforced the Australian attack on Mubo and the amphibious assault on Lae.

Australian Lieutenant General Edmund Herring. However, the effect of MacArthur's changes was to edge his loyal deputy, General Thomas Blamey, out of any position of power as Commander Allied Land Forces. Now, too, there existed the possibility that Blamey would be replaced by Krueger. Australia's Prime Minister, John Curtin, was not consulted about these changes, which were done with a marked degree of stealth. Their effect was obvious: the senior British Army officer in Australia at the time, Major General R. H. Dewing, wrote that MacArthur was "working steadily to exclude the Australians from any effective hand in the control of land or air operations or credit in them, except as a minor element in a U.S. show."

Yet at this stage of the war, the land forces available to MacArthur were still predominantly Australian, and the experiences of the 32nd Division outside Buna had shown that the American army forces, despite their technological superiority, were still basically untrained and unreliable in jungle operations.

In May 1943, Herring's New Guinea Force was given three tasks: the capture of Lae; the capture of Salamaua and Finschhafen; and the capture of Madang. Of the three objectives, Lae, with its harbour and airfield, was the most important. Salamaua was less so, but MacArthur's plan, based largely on Blamey's advice, was to maintain pressure against the Japanese there and disguise the real intentions of taking Lae. To the north, the objectives of Finschhafen and Madang were also vital because with Madang secured, MacArthur would have a safe left flank for operations against New Britain.

The capture of Salamaua and the Huon Peninsula were to be the responsibility of the

On July 1, American infantrymen patrol the Bitoi River mouth near Nassau Bay after a chaotic landing in which 19 landing craft were beached and wrecked. The Americans then spent a jittery pitch-black night under enemy fire.

Australian forces with some crucial specialised assistance from the Americans. Getting to within striking distance of Lae posed some problems, as an overland advance would have sapped the energies of the troops as well as providing the attacking force with a long and arduous resupply route. The alternative was to come by sea, but it was quite clear to Blamey and his planners that American landing craft to be used in any seaborne operation against Lae had to work from a base within 100 kilometres of the objective.

Nassau Bay, 23 kilometres south of Salamaua, was chosen as the most suitable site. The Americans landing there could link up with Australian 3rd Division forces, who had been operating for several months in the hills around Mubo in an effort to prevent enemy penetration of the Bulolo Valley through Mubo, Missim and the Markham areas. By mid-June the 2/6th

Battalion had made its way from Lababia Ridge to Nassau Bay in order to clear a path for the Americans, but on June 20 enemy forces attacked a forward company of the 2/6th and the Allies' plans for the area looked in jeopardy. However, the 2/6th's soldiers resisted and finally defeated the attacking force, enabling the Americans to come ashore at Nassau Bay early on June 30.

The landings were marred by heavy surf and a lack of experience in their operating methods; it became clear to Blamey's planners that more training was necessary before these difficult amphibious operations could be undertaken successfully. While these problems were being solved, planning was going ahead for the operations around Salamaua, but differing opinions between Australia's generals and MacArthur threw the campaign into confusion.

Major General Stan Savige had now taken

Corporal Leslie "Bull" Allen of 2/5th Battalion, carries an unconscious American to safety during the heavy fighting on Mount Tambu on July 30, 1943. Allen risked his life under intense fire to rescue 12 wounded.

command of the 3rd Division troops in the Wau area. He had a distinguished record from the First World War and had already commanded a brigade in the Middle East in this war. His plans to prevent the penetration of the Bulolo Valley and to advance on Salamaua were altered by Herring, who was privy to the greater strategy of Salamaua acting only as a diversion for the main Allied thrust against Lae. Blamey had written to Herring in clear enough terms: "The operation against Salamaua was to act as a magnet drawing reinforcements from Lae to that area."

Savige maintained he knew nothing of the diversionary plan, while Herring wrote later that Savige "rather went his own sweet way." Then MacArthur threw the tactics further into confusion when, after the Nassau Bay landings, he thought it would be possible to capture Salamaua quickly, offering the use of an American regiment to do so. It was obvious that MacArthur and Blamey were thinking differently about the operation. Its timing was of the essence: that Salamaua should not fall before the planned assault on Lae was essential.

Savige's troops had fought well and hard around Salamaua, but Blamey believed that the indecision about objectives and their sequence was jeopardising the entire operation. Even so, by mid-July all the Japanese positions around Mubo, including what had been one of their vital strongholds, the Pimple, had been found abandoned. The fighting was now concentrated in the high ground south of the Francisco River, which was vital for the Allies who wished to open a shorter sea route to the north through Tambu Bay. The enemy resisted the Australians' advances, but by the end of July troops of the 15th Brigade and the 2/3rd Independent Company captured the important northern reaches of the Bobdubi Ridge.

Herring had also decided to take Tambu Bay and to use the area to give artillery support to the 3rd Division. By the end of July, 26 guns were shelling the Japanese defences. The enemy's morale suffered severely, and so a force of 100 Japanese attempted to destroy the guns between Tambu Bay and Lake Salus. They were, however, soundly beaten. Now the Allies' attention turned to pockets of enemy soldiers occupying high ground between the southern end of Bobdubi Ridge and Tambu Bay, and especially on Mount Tambu. By mid-August they had been encircled, but the Japanese withdrew skilfully towards their last line of defence around Salamaua.

On August 24, the 29th Brigade relieved the 17th Brigade. The fresh troops of the 29th took over the area south of the Francisco River while the 15th Brigade maintained the pressure in the north, forcing the Japanese 51st Division to fight to the last. In the first days of September the Australians patrolled aggressively, ambushing the defenders many times and continuing to bombard Salamaua's defences. The Japanese had their backs to the wall.

Now the campaign came to fruition, for on September 4 the Allies made their assault on Lae, and four days later the Japanese troops in and around Salamaua were ordered to withdraw northwards through Lae and the Huon Peninsula. By September 10, the 15th Battalion began moves across the Francisco mouth towards Salamaua itself, but heavy rains and the flooding river slowed their advance, and the last remnants of the Japanese forces in the region were able to escape. The next day, the 42nd Battalion occupied Salamaua.

The fighting in the area from Wau to Salamaua had claimed more than 300 Australians killed and 750 wounded. American casualties mounted to 80 dead and 300 wounded. The Allies had, however, come out of the campaign far better than the Japanese, who had sustained heavy losses, but more importantly had been successfully diverted from the Allies' main thrust at Lae. The Salamaua magnet had worked magnificently.

Filmed by AIF cameraman Damien Parer, Private L.C. Mahon carries his gun in readiness for a commando assault on Timbered Knoll on July 29, 1943.

"My task was to convey the moment of truth when a soldier charges to kill or be killed"

DAMIEN PARER: EYEWITNESS TO BATTLE

In January 1940, a boyish 27-year-old Damien Parer slung his movie camera over his shoulder and boarded the troopship *Empress of Japan* bound for the Middle East. He was soon to become Australia's foremost photographer of the Second World War.

Born in 1912, Damien Parer gave up a calling to the priesthood after he discovered a passion for photography. Parer served his apprenticeship as a cameraman in Melbourne during the 1930s, working with famous Australian stills photographer Max Dupain and on camera crews at film-maker Charles Chauvel's studio. Though inexperienced, Parer was hired by the Commonwealth Department of Information (DOI) for their AIF film unit.

Parer soon earned puzzled admiration from the Diggers in the Middle East who regarded this devout but gutsy photographer as an amiable eccentric. Risking death to get the footage he wanted, Parer filmed the victorious Australian actions in the Libyan campaign until the fall of Benghazi. "My task," he said, "was to convey the moment of truth when a soldier charges to kill or be killed."

In April 1941, Parer took his camera to Greece where he recorded the 6th Division's tragic withdrawal. In June he was in Syria to film the 7th Division's victory over the Vichy French. Then, after a stint in the Desert Airforce and aboard the Tobruk Ferry Service, Parer returned home in March 1942 and was promptly dispatched to New Guinea.

Not content with filming Japanese Zero raids on Port Moresby, Parer joined Australian journalist Osmar White in June 1942 on a gruelling trip north, where commandos of Kanga Force faced the Japanese east of Wau. Parer returned to Moresby in mid-August, then he immediately headed up the Kokoda Trail where the 39th Battalion was desperately holding the enemy. Soon the Australians were in retreat, and a gaunt Parer, as starved and ill as the troops he filmed, doggedly recorded their fight back to Ioribaiwa Ridge. The newsreel film that combined all this hard-won footage, *Kokoda Front Line*, was released worldwide and received an Oscar for best documentary.

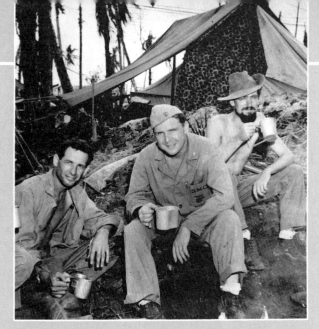

Photographed only weeks before his death, Damien Parer (left) brews up a billy of tea for American marines on Guam.

Parer followed this success with two more stunning war documentaries from Timor and the Battle of the Bismarck Sea. But Parer's greatest film was to come: *Assault on Salamaua*. From June to August 1943, Parer lived with Australian infantrymen as they fought bloody battles, ridge by ridge, from Mubo to Salamaua. The film's highlight is an attack on Timbered Knoll carried out by Lieutenant Johnny Lewin's platoon of the 2/3rd Independent Company on July 29, 1943. The soldiers of that campaign honoured the brave cameraman by naming a nearby battlefield "Parer's Bowl". Parer later returned the compliment, observing: "It is a privilege to be a war photographer when you have the honour to film men of the AIF."

Sadly it was to be Parer's last film of Australians. Fed up with strictures imposed by the DOI, Parer accepted an offer with Paramount News in August 1943. He went on to film the American invasions at Cape Gloucester, the Admiralty Islands and Guam, earning the same respect and affection from U.S. marines as he had from the Diggers. During action on Peleliu Island on September 20, 1944, Damien Parer's luck ran out. Crouching behind a tank to get a close-up of an infantry assault on a Japanese pillbox, Parer was cut down by machine-gun fire.

One of the finest and bravest of his profession, Damien Parer's commitment to his art showed in his willingness to share the soldiers' dangers and misery. His films did not glamorise warfare, but celebrated the courage of the individual Australian soldier in battle.

During an attack on Bobdubi Ridge, Private W. Johnson of the 58/59th Battalion, temporarily blinded by a grenade wound to the head, is escorted back to a dressing station on July 13, 1943, by Sergeant George Ayre.

Left: A commando of 2/3rd Independent Company races through kunai grass to report to his platoon commander Lieutenant Johnny Lewin. Top: Lewin (left) is shown an alternative route up a steep razorback spur to Timbered Knoll. Despite a preliminary artillery and mortar barrage to soften up enemy positions, two sections had been pinned down by machine-gun fire. Now, with Parer close behind, Lewin led a section up the spur while grenades were hurled forward with deadly effect. Above: Japanese dead sprawl in pillboxes and foxholes on the knoll after the enemy withdrawal.

prayerbook, while Lieutenant Johnny Lewin stands grim-faced on his other side.

4

TAKING THE HUON PENINSULA

Australia's 7th and 9th Divisions pounced in a masterful two-pronged attack on the large Japanese base at Lae, causing the enemy to flee into the mountains. Then the 9th struck at Finschhafen while the 7th battled over the Finisterre Range to cut off the desperate Japanese retreat.

With Japan's troops held up successfully inside their shrinking Salamaua perimeter, the Allies' hopes in eastern New Guinea began to unfold according to plan. The next phase of MacArthur's and Blamey's operations against the Huon Peninsula was now ready to be launched. Australian forces were to capture the township of Lae with its good harbour and airfield, the Markham Valley which stretched northwest into the Ramu Valley forming an inland route south of the Finisterre Range to and from Madang, and finally the Huon Peninsula coastline itself, fronting the vital sea lanes to the east.

MacArthur needed the whole area secured before he could make any further moves. His northwards thrust would now isolate the major Japanese garrisons rather than actually engage them in costly combat. Blamey, in charge of land operations, was also keen to have the area under his firm control. Once Lae was taken, resupply of troops operating in the hinterland would be easier; as well, new airfields could be built in the Markham Valley so that fighters and

George Allen's sandstone "Jungle Patrol" commemorates the grim courage and vigilance of Australian jungle-fighters.

bombers could support the ground operations. Blamey wrote: "Each forward move of air bases meant an increase in the range of our fighter planes and consequently an increase in the area in which transport planes supplying our troops could be operated. To get to airfields further and further foward was thus the dominant aim of both land and air forces."

Blamey took command of the operations towards Lae himself. The planning and preparation had taken months, particularly as the 9th Division, recently returned from the Middle East after its splendid participation in the battle of El Alamein, was to be involved. Now led by Major General George Wootten, the 9th had to be retrained in amphibious and jungle operations. They would be carried to beaches east of Lae by an American amphibious force commanded by Rear Admiral Daniel E. Barbey. Once ashore the Australian veterans were to advance quickly towards Lae.

At the same time Major General George Vasey's 7th Division was entrusted with airborne operations in the Markham Valley. Vasey planned to capture the old Nadzab airstrip using American paratroopers of the 503rd Infantry Parachute Regiment. Once these soldiers had seized the airfield, Vasey planned to move in engineers and pioneers to smooth out any damage to the landing surface, and then fly in the rest of his division. The 7th's role would be to prevent Japanese reinforcements from the Upper Markham and Ramu valleys reaching the 11,000 enemy troops already in the Lae-Salamaua area. As well, the Australians were to advance on Lae from the northwest.

The first AIF troops to be landed in these renewed offensives were Brigadier Victor Windeyer's 20th Brigade, who would form the initial wave at the beaches east of Lae. Windeyer, a prominent Sydney lawyer who had commanded a South Australian battalion in the Middle East, was to lead the Australian Army's first amphibious operation since Gallipoli; it was also one of the major Allied amphibious operations thus far in the Pacific. Aboard the 100-vessel convoy Windeyer's men were awake

early on the morning of September 4. Thanks to the Americans they breakfasted well on steak and eggs, coffee and tea; it was a welcome change from the stew, bully beef, and herrings in tomato sauce that had been their staple rations so far. The desert veterans of the 9th checked their weapons, tightened their webbing straps and peered anxiously through the lifting gloom for a glimpse of the New Guinea coast. As dawn broke, the imposing convoy was steaming westwards along the southern coast of the Huon Gulf.

The 9th Division was an outstanding formation with a splendid spirit forged in Tobruk and at El Alamein. In the desert the men of the 9th had developed the disconcerting habit of howling like dogs. Now, in the grey half-light of the brief tropical dawn, they began to howl once more, the woeful sounds adding to the ships' cacophony. "The dog yelps and howls helped to relieve the tension we all felt," recalled Private Ron Jones of the 2/15th Battalion.

At 6.18 am the landing barges were lowered and the heavily laden infantrymen began to clamber into them. Five destroyers began shelling suspected Japanese positions on the shoreline, sweeping the fire up and down the beach. In the barges the soldiers fixed bayonets, and listened to the bombardment in awe: even the desert veterans who had heard the mighty artillery before Alamein were impressed. The same occurred at nearby beaches as the barges headed off in perfect line and formation. The first wave hit the shore, and gun crews on the barges raked the fringe of the jungle with fire a few seconds before landing. The Australians in the first wave were fortunate that they struck no enemy opposition on the beach, and the men moved quickly to their allotted tasks. As the first companies filed ashore they were followed by American shore battalion specialists with their markers to guide the successive waves of landing troops. Next came heavy bulldozers and tractors, and heavy wire mesh to help wheeled vehicles across the soft sand. As the Americans worked feverishly on the shore, the Australian infantry pushed inland. The entire operation

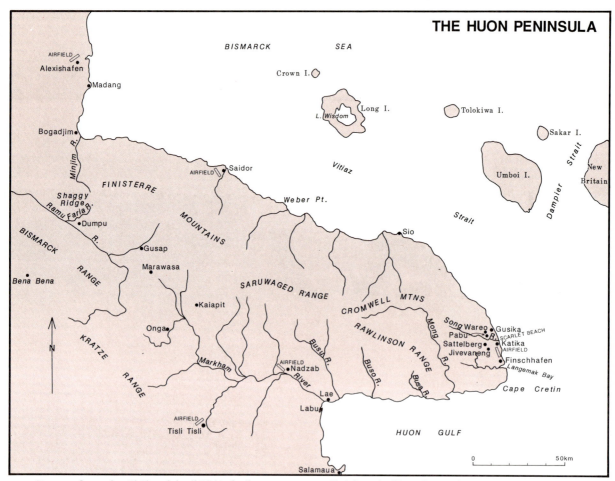

THE HUON PENINSULA

Between September 1943 and April 1944, the Japanese were expelled from the Huon Peninsula. The Australians captured Lae and Finschhafen on the coast, and pushed through the Markham and Ramu valleys and over the Finisterre Ranges.

was going more smoothly than Wootten and Windeyer had dared hope.

Japanese resistance so far had been very light. In the past month Japan's air strength had been savagely cut by massive Allied raids on the enemy's Wewak airbase and at fields in New Britain, ensuring that interference at these crucial landings would be minimal. But disaster struck the fifth wave when it was still 1,000 metres offshore. Suddenly nine Japanese aircraft appeared, strafing and bombing the landing craft. Casualties were fortunately small, although the tactical headquarters of the 23rd Battalion suffered a setback when a bomb landed just forward of its landing craft's bridge, killing the commanding officer and one company commander.

By 10.30 am, all the troops of the 20th Brigade were ashore along with 1,500 tonnes of their stores. The men soon headed inland; Major General Wootten was concerned that the Japanese might soon react to the landings and

organise quick defensive positions on the eastern side of the Busu River, the largest of five rivers and many streams between the landing beaches and Lae itself. Within 36 hours of the first soldiers setting foot, Wootten had his entire division on land ready to head for Lae.

The second prong of the advance was an airborne landing in the Markham Valley by the Australian 7th Division. Before the Australians could fly into the rudimentary Markham airfield, however, the strip and its ground approaches had first to be secured by native troops of the Papuan Infantry Battalion, who had made their way to the area overland, and by a regiment of American paratroopers. The Americans had no artillery so Australian gunners were asked to volunteer for the job, which to them was described as a special "training mission". The gunners were untrained in parachuting, although some of them did have one practice drop before the potentially hazardous operation.

After Australian assault troops hit the beaches east of Lae on September 4, 1943, a U.S. shore battalion from Admiral Barbey's amphibious force lays metal strips for road-building vehicles, and unloads stores from enormous landing ships.

The Americans, who were to supply all of the aircraft for the operation, were worried about Japanese fighters attacking the slow and vulnerable DC-3 transports. The U.S. air commander, General George C. Kenney, assigned more than 100 fighter aircraft, mostly American but with a sprinkling of Australian fighters, to provide a protective shield for the lumbering transports. As well, Kenney ordered six squadrons of specially rigged American B-25 bombers, each fitted with eight .50 calibre machine-guns in its nose and 60 fragmentation bombs in each of its bomb bays. These aircraft would spray the dropping zone just minutes before the drop.

The drop went perfectly as stick after stick quickly left their aircraft and descended to the field. And again the smoothness of the operation was helped immeasurably by the absence of Japanese opposition. The Americans suffered only three casualties that day. The Australian gunners, despite their lack of training, suffered only a few bruises and sprains. By the evening of September 5, they and the waiting troops of the Papuan Infantry Battalion were secure on the Nadzab airfield awaiting the arrival of the 7th Division.

When they arrived the airstrip had been prepared and the division's supplies readied. It was, wrote one soldier, a "rough-looking burnt clearing on which the descending planes were playing a game of 'follow my leader'. In a whirlwind of black dust they jolted down the short runway. A litter of stores was piled on either side in untidy heaps, and long lines of troops accompanied by native luggage porters trekked Indian file into the jungle."

Although the incoming troops arrived with little incident, one of Vasey's battalions was tragically struck down before it had even left for the fighting. On September 7 an American bomber ploughed into the trucks of the 2/33rd Battalion and the 158th General Transport Company while the Diggers were waiting to fly

In a breathtaking display of precision flying, 100 Douglas transport planes sweep low to drop paratroops of the 503rd American Parachute Infantry

Regiment and Australian 2/14th Field Regiment onto Nadzab airfield. The strip was ringed by smoke screens laid down by escorting fighters.

out of an airfield near Port Moresby. It was one of the greatest single losses of Australian soldiers in World War II; 59 died and 92 were injured. The survivors had no time for grieving, and were flown out to join the Australian thrust down the Markham Valley.

At the same time, the leading elements of the 9th Division had closed up to the Japanese outside Lae, but their advance was impeded by torrential rain slowing the troops' movement and swelling the already wide and formidable Busu River. Wootten had one of his brigades on the coast, the other about seven kilometres inland. On each route, the going was severely restricted by the terrain. Jeep tracks became impassable and once again resupply became a quartermaster's nightmare.

The absence of bridging to build crossings over the Busu worried the Australians. Although under fire from pockets of determined Japanese, the infantry fashioned makeshift craft to carry them across. But without bridges, and with the tracks severely affected by the rain, the movement forward of essential supplies was limited. Both Australian brigades had reached the Busu River on September 8, and the next day the 2/28th Battalion forced their way across its mouth after the enemy had been engaged heavily with field artillery and mortar fire. Upriver, the 26th Brigade battled on, finally crossing the Busu on September 14.

To the west, the 2/25th Battalion led the 7th Division's advance down the Markham Valley Road to Lae, with the 2/2nd Pioneers securing the right flank along the northern bank of the river, and the 24th Battalion guarding Markham Point to stop enemy troops coming from the south. Pockets of Japanese troops now made their stand at a series of plantations along the Lae road, but the 2/25th, helped by artillery, pushed the enemy back. Resistance was increasing, and on the morning of September 13 a strongly entrenched force of Japanese marines was encountered at Whittaker's plantation, 12 kilometres out of Lae.

Two companies of the 2/25th now moved onto higher ground. The going was slow, but the men had for the first time walkie-talkie sets to keep in touch. As the country got tougher, the soldiers came down into the plantation itself, but Japanese fire pinned down the leading Australian sections. Another platoon was called in to encircle the Japanese, but the enemy held tenaciously to their posts, inflicting severe casualties on the leading 2/25th platoon.

One section leader had already been killed and another, Corporal W.H. Richards, had been wounded and was lying exposed on a small rise. Still, he did his best to direct fire at the Japanese machine-gun post that had stopped his men, but his own position was dangerously vulnerable. Behind him two privates, Richard Kelliher and J.H. Bickle, were pinned down in a depression. Concerned about his section leader, Kelliher turned to his mate and said, "I'd better go out and bring him in."

Kelliher then took the last of his and Bickle's grenades and tossed them at the enemy machine-gunners before grabbing a Bren gun and racing forward. He emptied the Bren's magazine, but was unable to get to Richards. Kelliher returned for more ammunition, then turned straight around and crawled back out into the fray, firing from the ground until he had finished off the Japanese post. Fire now came from another enemy position, but Kelliher was able to grab Richards and drag him to safety. For his actions, Kelliher was awarded the Victoria Cross. It had been a treacherous day's fighting: the 2/25th had lost 10 killed and 16 wounded, but the flanking platoon that had gone out earlier had captured a local enemy head-quarters, allowing the Australians to move on towards Lae.

Fortunately, the men of the 9th Division had little fighting to do east of Lae. General Adachi, commanding the Japanese forces, initially had been misled by the pressure kept on Salamaua. Now he realised that with the 7th Division moving down the Markham Valley, and the 9th Division closing in from the east, his position at Lae was becoming increasingly untenable. He sought permission to withdraw across the Finisterre mountains to the northeast coast.

Having forced the enemy to abandon Lae, 9th Division troops hotly pursue retreating Japanese up the Buso River valley.
While the 9th Division prepared for another coastal assault, the 7th encountered fierce resistance in the hinterland.

Adachi's superior, General Imamura, agreed — so long as the harbour at Finschhafen was held and protected, and so long as Adachi's forces could continue to dominate the Ramu Valley.

The first major body of Japanese troops had already begun to leave Lae as the Australians were still struggling across the Busu. By now the Japanese were beginning to lose some of that closeknit cohesion and fighting spirit that had made them such formidable enemies. As they crossed over the ranges to the north of Lae, whole battalions flung down their equipment. Artillery was abandoned and discipline broke down. Many Japanese were severely ill.

In contrast, the Australians were highly spirited; now they could see that they had the Japanese on the run. In the 7th Division George Vasey kept the pressure on his troops, ever thrusting forward. By September 15 they had overcome strong defences and Japanese artillery fire around another plantation closer to Lae, and the next morning the 25th Brigade entered the town without opposition after it had been cleared by Allied bombers. Its precincts, however, were still unsafe as the 9th Division was pummelling the area with artillery. The 9th had occupied the region between Lae and the

Busu River with little effort, and was itself preparing to enter the township. The shelling ceased by early afternoon after a message finally got through, and both divisions now joined in the occupation.

Lae had fallen with remarkably little fighting, and much sooner than Allied planners had expected. Now Blamey could continue to apply the pressure, pushing along the coast of the Huon Peninsula. If the Vitiaz Strait could be secured, the American 6th Army would have a safe flank for the next part of the Allies' island-hopping campaign. An important objective for the Australians was the capture of the Finschhafen air and naval base, protected by a Japanese force that had been estimated variously between 350 and 4000. Despite such vague intelligence the task was given to Windeyer's 20th Brigade, which by now had developed an enviable career in amphibious warfare. Its expertise was clear from the speed with which Windeyer's staff organised the operation: the planning and orders were done in 48 hours; the landings, to be carried out on beaches 10 kilometres north of Finschhafen, were to go ahead within four days.

Realising that the Japanese were likely to 119

At dawn on September 22, 1943, Australian troops wade ashore at Scarlet Beach, north of the enemy stronghold at Finschhafen. In a confused amphibious landing, some troops were dropped at heavily defended points wide of the target.

defend this region with more ferocity than they had shown at Lae, Windeyer wanted two battalions landing on the shore at the same time. Despite the planning, the operation was not as smooth as the previous amphibious landings; now, on the run into Scarlet Beach on September 22, the American landing-craft commanders became confused and the Australian troops were dropped off at the wrong spots. Here, too, they faced one of the most difficult of all military operations: an opposed landing. The Japanese were waiting for them.

Still, the Australians came ashore calmly, forming themselves into scratch forces to destroy the opposing Japanese machine-guns before going in search of their parent battalions. Despite bitter early fighting, by dusk most of Windeyer's brigade was well inland.

The key to the Finschhafen area was the towering peak of Sattelberg. Inland from Scarlet Beach and northwest from the Finschhafen township, Sattelberg rose 1,000 metres above the countryside. Lutheran settlers had built a fine mission on the imposing peak, but now the Japanese commanded its heights. It could not be taken without first securing Finschhafen itself, and Windeyer was perturbed that just one brigade was not sufficient for the task. Rather than commit his forces, lose heavily and then be forced to ask for reinforcements, Windeyer suggested that the remainder of the division be deployed. He was told bluntly that an American assessment of the enemy at Finschhafen was such that he would not need extra troops. In fact, MacArthur's staff had refused to make available additional landing craft to carry more Australians forward, but after much pressure sufficient landing craft were released by the Americans to carry forward an additional battalion to Windeyer.

When the Australians landed, almost all the 4,000 Japanese troops around Finschhafen were concentrated on the south coast and at Sattelberg. The plan of the Japanese commanders, Generals Adachi and Yamada, was simple and bold: attack back towards the advancing Australians, seize the original beachhead and cut the force in half. It was precisely this kind of aggressive action which Windeyer feared — and which had been discounted by GHQ in Port Moresby.

As the American planners pondered the situation General Adachi moved quickly, rushing his 20th Division to the area. But before they arrived Yamada placed a force of marines north of Finschhafen, and in the last days of September they engaged the advancing Diggers in a bitter fight which dramatically slowed the Australian 20th Brigade's momentum. As well, Windeyer had to contend with torrential rain which slowed his resupplies moving forward and forced him to divert valuable fighting troops to carrying duties. He simply did not have enough soldiers to capture both Finschhafen and Sattelberg.

On the western thrust towards Sattelberg one company of the reinforcing 2/43rd Battalion, protecting forward on the road to the Japanese stronghold, was cut off early in the morning of October 1, and over the next few days it was attacked repeatedly by the enemy. The Australians, however, survived by simple

dogged defence. Towards Finschhafen the Japanese were resisting bitterly on that first day of October, but Allied airstrikes and artillery bombardment softened up the defences enough to allow the 2/13th to break through after heavy fighting. The Australians were unable to make it all the way to their main objective, the township of Finschhafen, but the Japanese had suffered heavily in the battle and began to evacuate the area; the Australian 22nd Battalion, a militia unit moving overland from Lae to join the Finschhafen battle, came upon abandoned enemy weapon pits as it approached. The next day Windeyer's troops occupied the village and harbour of Finschhafen.

From the landings at Scarlet Beach 11 days before, the Australians had suffered 358 casualties, of whom 73 had been killed in action. Japan's losses were much heavier; more than 100 marines had been killed on October 1 alone. And although Finschhafen had been captured, it was by no means secure. Australian Intelligence was receiving disturbing reports of a Japanese buildup around Sattelberg.

Windeyer wrote later that "to secure the gains

it would be necessary to continue the offensive and get possession of Sattelberg as quickly as possible." His orders were to advance north along the Huon Peninsula coast as far as Sio, but to do so he had to capture a long spur of high ground running from Wareo to the coast at Gusika; Sattelberg dominated that spur's western flank. The imposing peak would have to be captured.

But the Japanese themselves were intent on holding this region. By October 3 they had begun to threaten the still vulnerable beach-head from the north. By this stage it was clear to GHQ that Windeyer's original assessment of the Japanese intentions was correct, and American landing craft were made available to reinforce the Australians. As well, Wootten's divisional headquarters moved forward to take over responsibility for the area from Windeyer. But by October 11, Wootten still had only two of his three brigades. Now it was to be a race to see who struck first: Wootten preparing for his divisional attack on Sattelberg, or the Japanese with a counter-offensive to push the Australians back into the sea.

Through the early weeks of October the signs of an impending Japanese attack were clear. Intercepted radio messages gave a clue to the intentions, although without detail of the nature or direction of the attack. Then, in a marvellous stroke of luck for the Australians, a copy of the Japanese operation order for the counter-attack was captured and translated. It indicated a three-phase operation: a diversion from the north using artillery and infantry; a seaborne landing against the Australians on Scarlet Beach; and a main attack along the axis of the Sattelberg road and from the north.

Around Finschhafen and towards the towering height of Sattelberg, Australians watched and waited. Down at platoon and section level, in the sopping weapon pits and under damp tent-shelters, the Diggers knew what was happening and what was likely to happen. Wootten's still understrength division was spread out over a large area. He had positioned his troops for an area defence, reasoning that it would be better to fight from prepared positions and let the Japanese spend their resources in attack. Then, when the thrust had been blunted, the Australians could move onto the offensive. North and west of Scarlet Beach the 2/3rd Pioneer Battalion held two separate areas, with the 2/28th holding vital ground near the beach itself and the all-important beach dumps. To the south and west, the 2/43rd, the 2/17th and the 2/15th covered the track leading to the coast from Sattelberg while about eight kilometres south around Langemak Bay, Wootten had placed the 2/32nd Battalion, the 2/13th and the militia 22nd Battalion.

The first Japanese assault fell on the 2/17th Battalion astride the track at Jivevaneng on the morning of October 16, but this was held without much difficulty. At 3 o'clock the following morning the Japanese bombed Finschhafen as a preliminary to a seaborne attack by about 70 troops at the northern end of Scarlet Beach. In the darkness three Japanese barges approached the shore, but they were met by a strong force and were well beaten.

So far the Japanese counter had proved ineffective, and it was now optimistically thought that the enemy force was no match for the well-prepared defenders. Such bravado soon appeared misplaced when troops of the Japanese 79th Regiment, coming down from the north, moved silently and swiftly through the positions of the 2/3rd Pioneers inland from the beach. After fierce clashes with Australian patrols and bitter fighting around the pioneers' headquarters, a few Australians withdrew, leaving the northern flank perilously open. The Japanese were within 3,000 metres of Scarlet Beach itself, and on dominating ground. Now the 2/28th Battalion received the brunt of the offensive, and the Diggers gamely defended the vital coast road and the beach itself.

In the light of the strong Japanese thrust, Wootten requested his other brigade, the 26th, which was still in Lae. Its movement was given priority and MacArthur ordered the navy and airforce to assist in its rapid deployment.

That night, however, the Japanese did not press their attack forward; possibly they were experiencing supply problems. Sensing that the enemy had lost its momentum, Wootten ordered his division to "resume the offensive immediately." The positions lost over the previous 24 hours were to be taken and, with the assistance of additional troops, they would then head for Sattelberg.

But again the Japanese struck first. While the Australians were preparing to move forward, the 2/28th was hit by a determined Japanese assault aimed at getting to the sea and splitting the defenders' positions. The 2/43rd Battalion was also forced back, pulling out at night to new positions on the northern approaches to the beachhead. No sooner had it arrived and was digging-in than the Japanese hit. The high kunai grass and thick jungle were making infiltration between Australian positions easy, and coordination of the defence extremely difficult. For the next few days neither side could make significant progress; the offensive had petered out into bitter patrol clashes or repeated Japanese assaults against increasingly better-prepared Australian positions.

The beachhead was secured, but the Japanese had separated the two Australian brigades. And, although the enemy had established a road-block east of the 2/17th's position at Jivevaneng, cutting the battalion off, the Australians held on gamely to that post. Their desperate defence began to pay off, and by October 19 the Japanese were looking spent. The next night, Wootten's long-awaited reinforcements, the 26th Brigade under Brigadier D.A. Whitehead, and a squadron of tanks, arrived at Langemak Bay. The Japanese had lost the initiative and they soon withdrew. The battle had cost 49 Australians killed and an estimated 1,500 Japanese casualties.

Once Finschhafen and its approaches were

Matilda tanks, supporting the 26th Brigade, lumber up a narrow track to Sattelberg. Engineers bulldozed and built tank paths through the rough country around Sattelberg plateau, but the heights were finally won by dogged infantry assaults.

again secure, Wootten launched the offensive which he had planned before the Japanese counter-attack. The freshly arrived brigade and the tanks were set to clear the enemy from Sattelberg while the brigade in the north and the one in the centre, the 20th, would continue patrolling aggressively as a disguise. On November 16, the 2/48th captured the start line for the Sattelberg attack, a ridge west of Jivevaneng; the following day it began to move forward supported by the tanks.

Once again the tanks would make a decisive contribution to the coming battle. The tank squadron, commanded by Major Sam Horden, had developed effective tactics for working with the infantry. A troop of tanks, three or four depending on availability, would join a company of infantry and a platoon of engineers. The role of the infantry was to protect the tanks in close country; the role of the tanks was to blast enemy pillboxes and bunkers, assisted by the combat engineers with the explosives. Horden's squadron and Whitehead's brigade were old comrades; they had been training solidly together at Milne Bay. Now they were to be put to the test.

For the young tank crews, the excitement of their first major action was high. With their Besa machine-guns they raked the trees ahead with 50-round bursts, where probably five or 10 rounds would have done. The Japanese battled tenaciously, holding key positions along the track. Only 450 metres was gained in the first morning, and the fighting continued similarly for seven more days. Even the tanks struggled precariously to almost the highest points, their solid upward slog aided by concerted Allied air attacks upon the Japanese hill positions.

Meanwhile the 24th Brigade was active on the Gusika-Wareo track. After occupying a wooded knoll at Pabu, less than two kilometres from the coast, troops of the 2/32nd Battalion withstood a massive artillery bombardment. The Japanese also launched two major counter-attacks upon the position, but the Australians resisted all that could be thrown at them. It was a major Allied success, because the seemingly unimportant

post in fact sat astride Japan's major inland supply route to Sattelberg. The peak's defenders were slowly being starved of vital rations and ammunition.

In front of Sattelberg itself, the 26th Brigade inched closer and closer to the enemy fortress, and by November 22 the 2/48th Battalion reached its southern slopes, less than a kilometre from the summit. The tanks now found the going too tough, unable to make it through a recent landslide. The assault was left in the infantry's hands, and finally Sergeant Tom "Diver" Derrick's platoon of the 2/48th gained a toehold on the heights against a fortress of positions that literally bristled with machine-guns. Derrick, who had been decorated for bravery at Tobruk, took a look at the ground and decided the task was almost suicidal: "Jap bunkers on top could fire down on us and drop grenades; a sticky position indeed. Decided to give it a go," he wrote. "The move off required great courage and nerve and not a single man hesitated. The slope was exceedingly steep and each man had to have assistance to get started on the climb."

Derrick's platoon had not made much progress when they were first fired on. He still thought the task was beyond him, and he sent a runner back to his company headquarters to say so; he lacked a firm base from which to assault the final objective. In the headquarters Derrick's superiors agreed. His platoon was ordered to pull out.

Then the battle changed. Two Japanese in a foxhole ahead stood up; they were immediately shot by one of Derrick's Bren gunners. "Things seemed to be coming our way," he wrote. "I refused to pull out and the boys were keen to go on with it." A further order to withdraw was ignored, but even though Derrick lacked the space to throw his whole platoon at the enemy he considered the situation "touch and go". The young sergeant led his men up the almost vertical spur, fighting grimly for every metre. They pulled themselves forward, hand over hand, with Derrick the inspiration.

On the night of November 24/25, the Japanese

Soldiers of the 8th Brigade ford a river at Weber Point in pursuit of Japanese troops fleeing from Finschhafen along the north New Guinea coast. The brigade was sent to relieve the battle-weary 9th Division.

After a long trek in sweltering heat through the kunai grasslands of the Markham Valley, 7th Division troops rest at a friendly village. The capture of airfields for airborne reinforcements and supplies strengthened this inland offensive.

fled their positions; they were desperately short of supplies and fearfully astonished by the Australians' dogged line of approach. Effectively Derrick and his platoon had put the defenders on Sattelberg finally to flight. For this remarkable feat of arms Tom Derrick was awarded the Victoria Cross. A later Japanese account described it as "especially tenacious".

The winning of Sattelberg was a major turning point for the Australians. With the loss of the key areas around Lae and Finschhafen, all the Japanese could do now was defend, and the Allies were able to advance around the coast and inland through the big valleys of the Huon Peninsula.

While the 9th Division had been occupied around Finschhafen, the 7th Division was working its way up the Markham and Ramu valleys heading northwest out of Lae towards Madang. These two valleys were the key to the mountainous inland route to and from Japan's New Guinea coastal bases. Japan's General Adachi had long held plans to establish a land line from Madang south over the Finisterre Range, through the Ramu and Markham valleys and on to Wau, where he would then head overland to Port Moresby. By mid-1943, however, Australian troops had been established in force around Bena Bena to check such a thrust and to secure an emergency airfield in support of the Huon Peninsula offensive.

After the Nadzab landings and the fall of Lae, the 7th Division and several of the independent companies moved up the valleys to establish more airfields both for the resupply of Allied ground troops and to provide bases for their tactical air support. Sporadic clashes with enemy units occurred and by October the 7th's commander, George Vasey, had concentrated his men between Dumpu and Marawasa. Vasey, however, made no major advances; the Australian general's responsibility was to protect the Ramu and Markham valleys from the Japanese while the air bases were being built. Nevertheless, he ordered a program of vigorous patrolling calculated to deny the

In December 1943, an Australian patrol clambers through deep mud on the higher slopes of the Finisterre Range, a precipitous mountain chain covered with dense rainforest and subject to almost daily deluges of rain.

Japanese information of the Australian positions and to keep the enemy off balance.

At first the Japanese did little to counter the Australian patrolling, but by early December Vasey's troops began to notice a difference in the reactions of the enemy. The 7th Division's left flank found themselves fighting bitterly. In the centre, the troops faced a dominating feature known as Shaggy Ridge, a razorback spur rising more than 1,500 metres covered in dense rainforest.

The ridge ran parallel to the upper Faria Valley and controlled the approaches from Dumpu. Although the Australians had already gained a foothold on the southern slopes of this spur, they found their way forward barred by a rocky outcrop known as the Pimple, which rose almost vertically from the narrow crest. On the lower slopes of Shaggy Ridge the Japanese had prepared defensive positions. By now the 2/16th Battalion's diarist, Captain Malcolm Uren, recalled almost every patrol was running into trouble, but the pressure was kept on the

Japanese. "Our orders were not to advance but merely to harass. These were both irksome and unhelpful to morale," Uren wrote. "The troops could see little value in accepting the hazard of patrol, driving the enemy out of positions and then retiring and permitting the enemy to walk back into them."

Vasey's orders, however, gave sufficient flexibility to try and take Shaggy Ridge. The task fell to 21st Brigade, and particularly to the 2/16th Battalion. Originally the attack was planned to go in before Christmas 1943, but the date was postponed to allow the troops time for celebrations. The 2/16th troops dined well on Christmas Day with turkey, ham, pudding, fruit and fresh cream.

The attack went in on December 27, against an estimated three platoons of Japanese. It was preceded by accurate bombing raids by American Kittyhawk and Australian Boomerang aircraft, and by heavy artillery fire. At 9 am precisely, the men of Lieutenant Arthur Geyton's 10 Platoon crossed the start line.

Giving the 18th Brigade a precarious toehold on Shaggy Ridge, 2/9th Battalion dig in on "Green Sniper's Knoll" after capturing it on January 22, 1944. The battalion held the position against vicious counter-attacks and mortar fire.

Ahead of the Australians was terrible terrain. In some places the incline was so steep that the Diggers had to haul themeselves up by hand; at other points they carried roughly improvised ladders. The Japanese commanded the slopes from where they could roll grenades down onto the Australians. It took Geyton's men nearly an hour to advance the few hundred metres to the Pimple, often along a track on the razorback so narrow that only one man could move at a time.

Geyton's men were relieved when another platoon pushed through to take over from them. Again the advance edged forward, each Australian acutely aware not only of the Japanese in front of him but the steep and treacherous slopes at the side. By midday the Australians held the heights and, in the distance, they could see the sea beyond Madang. The couple of companies involved had struggled relentlessly against a determined and well-prepared enemy, and although the Australian casualties were surprisingly light, the troops were exhausted and suffering from disease.

Vasey swapped his brigades around, bringing Brigadier Fred Chilton's 18th Brigade into the operations. Chilton planned an elaborate set of manoeuvres using all three of his battalions: the 2/9th along Shaggy Ridge itself, the 2/10th to its right, and the 2/12th on the left flank. The 2/10th proceeded along a northern saddle, diverting enemy attention from the two other battalions. Then the 2/9th slowly made its way along the ridge's razor-edged crest while the 2/12th crept up the steep sides, fighting off heavy opposition. Despite several counter-attacks, late in January 1944 the 18th Brigade captured the key to the enemy's hold on the ridge, Kankiryo Saddle, at the northern extremity of Shaggy Ridge, thus surrounding the Japanese. However, enemy forces continued to provide stiff resistance to the Australians in an effort to allow withdrawal of the 20th and the 51st Japanese Divisions around the coast. At the end of the month the Japanese,

still holding on north of Kankiryo, withdrew to the northwest, but the militia 15th Brigade relieving the 18th followed and after several clashes occupied Bogadjim in mid-April.

The Huon Peninsula campaign was finally closing. Other Australian militiamen were coming around the coast, chasing enemy units which had fled from Finschhafen north to Sio and on to Saidor. The Americans had also re-entered the New Guinea campaign, landing at Saidor in early January, but they let the escaping Japanese through their clutches and more than 8,000 enemy troops were able to flee further west to the Aitape-Wewak region. Soon the Americans and Australian militia coming over the Finisterres linked together, and on April 24 Madang fell without a fight. The Australians had recaptured the peninsula. The offensives that had opened in September 1943 had cost them 1,231 killed and 2,867 wounded. Japanese losses were estimated at 35,000.

While the Australian Army was finishing off what had been its largest campaign of the war, the Allied push to encircle and isolate Rabaul was achieved in March. Undertaken mainly by American forces but with Australian naval and airforce assistance, Japan's great Pacific base and its 100,000 troops were finally rendered useless. MacArthur now moved quickly along New Guinea's north coast, virtually cutting off the Japanese garrisons in the region. In the coming year, the Japanese were not given an opportunity to regroup; everywhere the pressure was kept on, either by Australians or by Americans. At the head of a vast and formidable war machine, MacArthur displayed a remarkable degree of flexibility, changing his plans to suit the strategic opportunities as they arose. But by September 1944 the future use of the Australian forces provided new and special problems for its commanders. MacArthur had the Philippines firmly in his sights, and the Australians were left to fight their own, very different battles.

"Our air boys are right on top and giving them hell"

With bomb doors still open, a Boston pulls away from a bombing run over the Japanese base at Hollandia village and Humboldt Bay.

ALLIED WINGS

Flight Lieutenant W.E. Newton VC.

While most RAAF aircrews served in the Middle East and European theatres, 31 Australian squadrons played a smaller but vital role in the Pacific with the United States Air Force. A large part of the RAAF's strength in this region was taken up in Australia's coastal defence, but several squadrons were involved in important actions in the Allied air offensive against the Japanese.

In late 1942, seven RAAF squadrons based in New Guinea were formed into No. 9 Operational Group and incorporated into General George C. Kenney's 5th American Air Force. They played an aggressive role harassing enemy supply lines and garrisons during the Japanese retreat from Kokoda, the Allied counter-attacks at Buna, Gona and Sanananda, and the Australian push towards Salamaua and Lae. During one daring low-level bombing run over Salamaua on March 18, Flight Lieutenant W.E. Newton was shot out of the sky, but he managed to bellyflop his plane onto the sea and swim safely ashore. He was captured and executed by the Japanese; for his actions Newton was awarded the only Victoria Cross received by an RAAF airman in the Pacific War.

As the Japanese attempted to reinforce the Salamaua and Lae areas in March, a strike wing of the 5th American Air Force, led into attack by RAAF Beaufighters, destroyed a Japanese troop convoy from Rabaul. This Battle of the Bismarck Sea was a resounding victory for Allied airpower; with Japan's air superiority now finished, the enemy had lost its means to reinforce New Guinea.

Meanwhile Australia's home defence had been strengthened in January 1943. Three squadrons of No. 1 Spitfire Wing under the command of ace fighter pilot, Wing Commander Clive Caldwell, soon tasted blood in dog-fights over Darwin in March.

The Allied airforces were now directed against Rabaul, and during July and August 1943, No. 9 Group RAAF, flying from airfields on Kiriwina and Goodenough islands, blockaded Japanese bases in New Britain in preparation for an Allied combined amphibious-airborne assault on the Lae-Nadzab region in September. In that month the Australian airmen were continually in the thick of the action with Boston and Beaufort bombing raids on Gasmata airstrip, New Britain, and Beaufighter sweeps of the Huon Gulf to destroy enemy barges. Praising the Australian and American pilots who supported the troops at Lae by fighting off Japanese air attacks, Lieutenant Colonel E. Macarthur Onslow, commanding the 2/2nd Machine-Gun Battalion, recorded in his diary: "Our air boys are right on top and giving them hell."

The full power of the 5th Air Force, including RAAF Beauforts and Beaufighters, was released on Rabaul, while Australian Kittyhawk and Spitfire squadrons supported American assaults in the Solomon and Admiralty Islands. By now the Japanese were reeling; the air war against Rabaul during 1943 and early 1944 was a major tactical defeat for the Japanese.

While No. 9 Group RAAF stayed as a garrison force in eastern New Guinea, the RAAF organised a second mobile task force, No. 10 Operational Group, to give defensive air cover to MacArthur's rapid push along the north coast. They moved to Aitape in April and Noemfoor Island in July. The time was fast approaching for an all-out invasion of the Philippines, and the final Allied thrust back to Japan itself.

In late 1942, Beaufighters of No. 30 Squadron RAAF based at Port Moresby soar over the Owen Stanley Range to strafe the retreating enemy.

JUST A SIDESHOW

While American airpower dominated the Pacific in 1944, Australia's role diminished. When MacArthur secured Morotai as a forward airbase in September and prepared for the invasion of the Philippines, he expected No. 10 Group RAAF to stay behind in New Guinea to support the Australian Army. Some RAAF squadrons did remain to help the Australian troops in the Aitape-Wewak, Bougainville and New Britain campaigns, but Australian Air Vice-Marshal W.D. Bostock protested to the U.S. Air Command, ensuring that the RAAF was given a more forward role. By October, No. 10 Group, reorganised as 1st Task Air Force and reassigned to the 13th American Air Force, was based at Morotai; it had grown rapidly to one attack wing, two fighter wings and two airfield construction wings under Australian veteran ace Air Commodore Harry Cobby.

The 1st TAF concentrated on harassing enemy garrisons in the Halmaheras, Celebes and on other islands bypassed by the American forces. But the Australian airmen soon became discontented. They regarded their mopping-up operations, though well planned and conducted, as costly and militarily unjustifiable. They resented the RAAF's part in what was being criticised as an "unnecessary war" being fought behind the main American thrust towards Japan. By April 1945, eight senior decorated fighter pilots including Group Captains C. Caldwell, J.L. Waddy and W.S. Arthur could stand no more, and in a concerted protest they offered their resignations.

Eventually the storm blew over, and the RAAF's Kittyhawks, Spitfires, Beaufighters, Mosquitos and Liberators went on to support Australian ground forces at Tarakan, Labuan, Brunei and Balikpapan in Borneo. Meanwhile, the Pacific war moved on towards Japan, ending quickly and unexpectedly. The RAAF had sustained heavy losses in men and machines: in the South-West Pacific area 3,342 died and 1,614 were injured. Their fighting spirit and sacrifice had, however, helped wrest control of the air from the Japanese and drive their Pacific forces into retreat.

Australian and American fighter planes appear like insects on a white coral airstrip

Squadron Leader John Waddy   *Squadron Leader Wilfred Arthur*   *Group Captain Clive Caldwell*

on Morotai island. Fifteen Allied aircraft were destroyed in an enemy bomber attack on Wama and Pitu airfields on the night of November 22, 1944.

Their silk parachutes crumpling, American paratroopers drop from Douglas aircraft among RAAF trucks and bulldozers on Kamiri airstrip. Australia's

No. 10 Operational Group was stationed on Noemfoor Island to repair runways and give fighter cover to the Americans.

5

MOPPING UP

As America dominated the quickening Allied push towards Japan, Australian forces were left to contain enemy garrisons on Bougainville, New Britain, around Wewak, and in Borneo. The campaigns were costly, but they established Australia in the region as Japan crumbled to defeat.

Ray Ewer's dignified bronze figure "Australian Infantryman" immortalises the young Australian warrior of the Pacific war.

By mid 1944 the war had moved away from the Australian forces in Papua and New Guinea. General MacArthur's SWPA forces had made rapid advances along New Guinea's northern coast, preparing for his long-awaited and much-heralded return to the Philippines, while in the Solomons American naval forces had pushed the enemy into the islands of Bougainville and up to New Britain. In the Central Pacific, American Admiral Chester Nimitz had moved his powerful naval group against the Marshall Islands and the giant Japanese base of Truk island in the east Carolines.

It was clear that Australia had little part in such progress, and was to take on a new role in the Pacific campaign. Australia's forces, however, were uncertain of their next move. Major Russell Lyons, an original AIF volunteer in 1939 and now serving on the 3rd Division headquarters, recalled, "The word was around that MacArthur had told Blamey that he didn't need Australian troops any longer and that, apart from garrison duties, the AIF could go home. These were the words we wanted to hear."

Australia's commanders, on the other hand, were itching to become more involved in the war. The Labor Government of Prime Minister John Curtin wanted to remain fighting for reasons of national interest. Curtin told the Commonwealth Prime Ministers' Conference in London in May 1944: "Australians wished to have a say in how the Pacific area was to be managed, and they realised that the extent of their say would be in proportion, not to the amount of wheat, meat or clothes they produced to support the forces of other nations, but to the amount of fighting they did."

Curtin and his commanders wanted to serve in two main areas: the territories Australia had lost in the initial 1942 Japanese thrust; and, for reasons of pride and influence, with America's front-line troops in the Philippines. Yet by the time Curtin had arrived home from the London conference, America had moved rapidly ahead in its plans to take back the Philippines. Fearful that the U.S. was quickly overshadowing Australia's influence in the SWPA, Curtin canvassed for a British naval contribution in the region to balance America's increasing power; the British Pacific Fleet came into being in November that year.

But the Americans were moving quicker than ever, thanks almost entirely to the remarkable job that had been done by Australian forces in New Guinea laying the initial groundwork for MacArthur's easy route to the northwest. Now the American general needed for his Philippine operations the six U.S. divisions holding on to Bougainville, New Britain, and around Aitape in northern New Guinea.

And so, far to the south of the main thrust of the Pacific war, these American formations were to be replaced by four Australian divisions. The AIF troops had been based for much of 1944 in Australia, regrouping, being reinforced, and maintaining fighting fitness. The Diggers of the II Australian Corps were now to fight in the northern Solomons, the 5th AIF Division was to go to New Britain, and the 6th Division to the Aitape-Wewak area.

The Australian soldiers had relieved the Americans on Bougainville by mid-December 1944. Up to then the Americans had subdued the Japanese, but no side dominated the island which had been originally occupied by the enemy in March and April 1942. The Japanese had built airfields there for fighter and bomber staging, but superior American firepower and air strength cut vital Japanese supply lines and eventually swung the balance against the occupying forces.

The Japanese strength was in the south, while the Americans had consolidated their position on Bougainville around Torokina, on the northern edge of Empress Augusta Bay on the western side of the island. The U.S. soldiers did not venture far from their well-prepared base, and in fact it was left to a battalion of Fijian infantry partaking in the Allied effort to do any long-range patrolling.

Effectively, the Americans and the Japanese were content with a "live and let live" policy. Starved of supplies, the Japanese established vegetable gardens and spent much of their energy tending them; when the Australians took over, only about 8,000 of the 40,000 Japanese on the island were available for fighting. Of the rest, about 14,000 were gardening or fishing, 6,000 were transporting the meagre supplies to scattered units, and 12,000 were sick.

As the Australian soldiers arrived on Bougainville they were astonished by the attitudes and the conditions of the Americans. At Jaba River, on the western side of the island, one Australian battalion took over in December 1944 and while the Americans were packing up to leave, the first Australian patrols prepared to cross the river into Japanese territory. "You're surely not going to send patrols over there," the Americans said in amazement. "There are Japs over there."

For the Australians the war was moving with a slower tempo than they had been used to. The Americans' interest in fighting on Bougainville was slight, with their focus and their all-important transport equipment having shifted further to the north. However, not all the

BOUGAINVILLE

Buka Island

Buka Passage

South Pacific Ocean

Buka
Bonis Peninsula
Bonis Tarlena
Porton

EMPEROR RANGE

BOUGAINVILLE ISLAND

Numa Numa

NUMA TRAIL

PEARL RIDGE

Torokina

CROWN PRINCE RANGE

Empress Augusta Bay

Jaba R.

Puriata R.

Solomon Sea

Slater's Knoll

BUIN Buin

N

0   50
Kilometres

Shortland Is.

Relieving U.S. troops by December 1944, Australian forces on Bougainville launched a major offensive, pushing the Japanese north to Buka Island, and down the south western coast.

largesse had gone — the Americans left behind refrigeration space, not to mention an ice-cream and soft-drink factory at Torokina. Even so, the Australian troops suffered light rations in December and January 1944.

Blamey had warned that operations should be of a "gradual nature" for he had no specific approval from the Australian Government for mounting an offensive. But, despite equipment shortages, Lieutenant General Savige, in charge of Australian troops on Bougainville, made it clear from the very beginning that he was not prepared to sit quietly behind defences and "live and let live". The Australian corps commander's primary task was the defence of the Torokina base, but Savige realised that he would have to deny access to Torokina along a trail across the island's girth, from Numa Numa on the east coast. As well, he would have to contend with enemy forces in the north. On December 23, 1944, Savige issued orders that would carry the war to the Japanese; the easy truce was now to be shattered.

Quite clearly, the decisive battle would have to be fought in the south of the island, while at the same time Savige would have to meet the Japanese force in the north and a threat posed by enemy troops occupying Pearl Ridge on the trail crossing the centre of the island. In the first major action of the Bougainville campaign, the Queenslanders of the 25th Battalion were sent in against the Japanese on Pearl Ridge. This attack was preceded by air attack from New Zealand fighter-bombers, but the narrowness of the track made it difficult for Lieutenant Colonel John McKinna's men of the 25th Battalion to manoeuvre.

One company, commanded by Lieutenant B. A. Shaw, had to move along a ridge only four metres wide where a huge bomb crater lay between them and the Japanese, who had covered the obstacle with machine-guns and mortars. At first the Australians tried to move around the flanks, but the Japanese sitting above rolled hand grenades down upon them. After eight hours of fighting, Shaw's company was still held up at the obstacle. McKinna ordered them to halt for the day and try again the next morning.

During that night the Japanese attacked, trying to dislodge the Australians from their precarious holds on the sides of the razorback ridge. The next morning McKinna's men tried again, this time with more success. By mid-afternoon they were on top of Pearl Ridge, from which they could see both sides of the island. In the process, however, they had defeated not just the 80 or 90 Japanese they had been told were there, but a battalion of well dug-in troops. For the first time the Australians realised that their Intelligence assessments of Japanese intentions might be slightly optimistic.

In the three months after Pearl Ridge was taken, the war on Bougainville settled down into deep patrolling operations. For Corporal Peter Medcalf, a rifleman in the 15th Battalion, this aspect of the jungle war turned his stomach with fear. "Step over the wire, leading the patrol out into the jungle. It was always like this," he said. "I wondered did the others feel the same? Fear of what was out there, 50 yards away, a mile away, in two minutes? An hour? I

THE AMERICAN FINALE

After the Allies' great battles in New Guinea, Australia's role in the direction of the Pacific war diminished. America pushed quickly ahead in its efforts to throw back Japan's forces from the South West Pacific Area, and with assistance from Australian naval and air forces, General Douglas MacArthur thrust northwestwards towards the Philippines.

He had been aiming all his command's power in that direction since the grand strategic plan for the Pacific was drawn up by the Allied Chiefs of Staff in January 1943. The Pacific theatre, under American operational command, was divided between General MacArthur's SWPA and Admiral Chester Nimitz's Central Pacific Area. Nimitz was given the task of preparing a thrust through the Central Pacific, which he considered to be the shortest and most effective route towards the Japanese homeland. MacArthur's first objective was to isolate and neutralise Japan's major base at Rabaul by driving through the Solomons and northeast New Guinea to encircle New Britain.

MacArthur's campaign went well, and once Australian troops had won the Huon Peninsula the door was open for the American general to move quickly along New Guinea's northern coastline. His forces landed at Saidor in January 1944, but they failed to cut off Japanese soldiers retreating westwards. By March, Rabaul had been cut off and 100,000 Japanese troops there were rendered inoperative. MacArthur immediately seized the Admiralty Islands to establish a naval base, and he went on to launch a spectacular series of American amphibious assaults at Aitape and Hollandia on April 22 followed by Wakde, Biak and Noemfoor islands. By the end of July his men had reached the tip of the Vogelkop, the westernmost "head" of New Guinea. Now the final stepping stones to the Philippines for MacArthur were Morotai island in the Halmaheras, and Peleliu island, which were taken by large amphibious forces in September.

Meanwhile Nimitz's westward thrust through the Central Pacific had begun in November 1943 with attacks on the Gilbert Islands, where the Japanese garrison on Tarawa fought to the death. The pattern was repeated throughout the Central

On December 7, 1944, U.S. 77th Division troops storm ashore at Ormoc Bay on Leyte island in the Philippines. The protracted Leyte battle against a stubborn garrison cost 4,000 American lives.

Pacific's islands: in February the Marshalls succumbed after a long fight and, in June, Nimitz unleashed his combined air-sea-land force on the Marianas. During the struggle for Saipan in June, Japan's carrier air-wing attempted a counter, but lost heavily in a showdown with its opposing carrier force on June 19 which the Americans jubilantly dubbed "The Great Marianas Turkey Shoot". More than 300 Japanese aircraft with their invaluable pilots were downed, drastically reducing Nippon's capabilities in the Central Pacific. Guam and Tinian islands were the next to fall by early August.

Having completed a wide-sweeping pincer movement through the central and southwest Pacific, MacArthur and Nimitz now stood poised to invade the Philippines. But Japan's remaining flyers based in Formosa attempted to halt the Americans' advances, and in a massed air attack on Nimitz's naval and sea-air forces in the Philippines Sea in early October the Japanese again lost hundreds of planes and virtually any remaining hope of concerted defence.

On October 20, Nimitz and MacArthur joined forces for a massive assault on Leyte island in the central Philippines. The Japanese

Combined Fleet, in an attempt to destroy the American beachhead, lost 26 warships and more than 10,000 sailors and airmen in the marathon naval Battle of Leyte Gulf. Now, between MacArthur and final victory in the Philippines stood around 250,000 enemy soldiers under General Yamashita, "the Tiger of Malaya" who had led the initial Japanese thrusts of 1942. An estimated 60,000 of them died holding Leyte until December 25. MacArthur moved on to Luzon, the Philippines' largest island and, after a bitterly resisted landing at Lingayen Gulf in January 1945, American ground forces were tied down to the end of the war in a long and bloody battle.

By the middle of that year, the thrust of the war had moved away from the larger islands and land masses of the west Pacific to the smaller islands that were Nimitz's responsibility to the east. The Pacific war was now primarily a naval campaign, and the admiral went on to fight America's costliest battles on Iwo Jima and Okinawa, at the enemy's southern doorstep. Japan's troops defended to the death their country's crumbling war effort, but hostilities were, without a doubt, nearing an inevitable yet chilling end.

would not feel the *Nambu* burst that hit me — no time to dodge, stomach cramping, sick."

All the time, the Australians were building up and preparing for the operations south along the coast towards the Japanese strength, where Savige's decisive battle would be fought. Along the way was a major obstacle, the Puriata River, at which Savige was convinced the Japanese would make a stand, attempting to delay his advance. Commandos of the 2/8th Independent Company, as part of Savige's corps, were moved upstream along the banks of the Puriata to protect the flanks of the main advance along the coastal swamps. But it soon became clear that the Japanese were not defending the Puriata. And so, on March 4, Lieutenant Colonel McKinna's 25th Battalion led an Australian advance over the river and engaged a Japanese rearguard holding high ground known as Slater's Knoll, astride the road to Buin. So far, all had gone relatively easily, but the Japanese tactics were about to change: they now took on the advancing Australians with heavy artillery fire, forcing the forward companies of the 25th Battalion to dig in only a few hundred metres from the source of the shelling.

Towards the end of the month the Australians found themselves surrounded by the Japanese, cut off and low on both food and water. Then, on March 31, a troop of heavy Matilda tanks were brought forward to regain the initiative. They rolled towards the besieged companies, with infantry advancing as well on both sides of the tanks. The Japanese were forced back, suffering heavily, but in the next few days they threw in several strong counter-attacks only to be stopped close to the Australians' positions. After a week of solid fighting, the Japanese attempted one last-ditch attack in the early morning of April 5, but they were stopped literally metres from the dug-in Australians. It was now time for the tanks to use their weight again, and that afternoon they turned the battle around. Few Japanese survived, and the next day the Queenslanders of the 25th counted nearly 300 dead Japanese around the Slater's Knoll position.

The tanks had made the critical difference, but despite this there were still some senior army officers who thought that tanks had no place in the tropical battlefields such as Bougainville. Tanks, despite the formation of the Armoured Division for two years, were in short supply. Yet one month after this battle, an Australian officer discovered 160 American tanks left to rust on an island just north of Guadalcanal. Of these tanks, 140 had never been used; had they been available for the fighting on Bougainville they would have made an enormous difference to the long, slow slog down the coast.

Shortages of all kinds impeded the Australians as they advanced both to the north and south of the main base at Torokina. The sea, a vulnerable flank for the Japanese about which they could do very little, was an obvious way of moving troops and avoiding the difficult going along the coastal swamps. Yet here, too, the Australians were desperately short of vital landing craft.

Such problems showed up in an operation on the northern coast when the Australians attempted to land from the sea to get behind the Japanese. On June 8, a company of the 31st/51st Battalion, reinforced until it contained nearly 200 men, was ordered to go in against a reported group of 100 Japanese in positions around Porton coconut plantation. This force, commanded by Captain H. C. Downs, was to land by night, secure a beachhead, then move quickly inland to link up with another force moving overland. The first wave of three landing craft got ashore successfully against little opposition, but as the second wave landed, the Japanese defenders opened fire with heavy machine-guns and artillery. The Australians were caught in the open. All day on June 8, Downs's force held on to a narrow beachhead under heavy Japanese fire, and that night the Japanese, by now well-reinforced, attacked repeatedly in an effort to throw the Australians back into the sea. Those attacks failed, but that did not stop the Japanese from attacking again on the morning of June 9. Still the Australians held on.

Downs's situation was becoming desperate. Late that afternoon, three landing craft made the perilous journey in to the Australians in an effort to get the survivors off the shore. Thanks to the efforts of the landing-craft crews, every Australian left alive on the beach was disembarked, but two of the landing craft became firmly stuck on coral reefs near the beach. Again the Australians were under fire.

That night one of the barges floated free, but the second was so heavily laden with wounded, and half-filled with water, that it remained firmly wedged on the reef. The Japanese continued to pepper the Australians with fire, and in efforts to escape several Australians were swept overboard, including Downs, who was never recovered. Some swam out to sea — but sharks had been seen in the area. Several Japanese soldiers then swam out to the raft and attempted to throw grenades on board, but they

were shot at close range by Australians on board. The Japanese tried another ploy. "At 0400 a lone Jap swam around the barge calling out, 'I am Johnson, come and help me,' and 'I am blind and wounded.' It was an obvious Jap ruse and easily detected as another was heard on the shore giving out orders and telling the swimmer what to say," Private Bill Crawford recalled. "The swimmer began jabbering violently in Japanese, and was apparently moving back when he was seized by a shark."

The Australians endured continual harassment, and many of the men were reduced to delirium from lack of sleep and the never-ending pounding of enemy fire. Finally, on June 11, they were rescued. Their losses were great: of the 190 men who had gone into the attack, 23 had been killed and 106 wounded.

The Japanese remained in strength in the Porton plantation, but they were increasingly

A Matilda tank of the 2/4th Armoured Regiment is towed by a bulldozer across the Puriata River, Bougainville, on March 30, 1945. Tanks were rushed forward to support the besieged 25th Brigade at Slater's Knoll.

hemmed into a small area of the Bonis Peninsula and Buka Island in the north. In the south they had withdrawn to a concentrated area of about 50 kilometres by 25 kilometres. Although Australian Intelligence put the number of Japanese on the island at around 20,000, there were in fact 24,000.

The Australian losses were a bitter blow to the Diggers, whose strength and enthusiasm was beginning to be sapped by the tempo of the action. They realised that their fighting could have little influence on the outcome of the Pacific war; they also realised that, without the direct support of the massive American war machine, they would be condemned to fighting useless campaigns with insufficient resources. Major Russell Lyons recalled: "For me the war stood still. I just couldn't believe it. Men who had served faithfully a cause for years were exposed to death once more when they should have been reunited with the living."

The so-called "mopping-up campaigns" received little recognition at home. Rarely was there any mention of Bougainville in Australia's newspapers, and the men left doing the fighting were bitter and resentful about what they saw as the indifference of the authorities and the press. Nearly two divisions had been fighting on the island for more than six months against a larger enemy force than had fought in New Guinea in 1942 and 1943. But the government appeared determined to hide the fact, recalled Corporal Peter Medcalf. "It seemed to us the war had moved north to Borneo and the Philippines. We begrudged every casualty, and the end seemed a long way off."

Much the same story unfolded to the west, around Aitape and Wewak in northern New Guinea. The Aitape-Wewak battles were fought by Australians of the 6th Division AIF, which still included some of the men who had volunteered for this splendidly elite force in 1939. Here the Australians took over from the Americans in October 1944 but shipping shortages delayed the arrival of many troops, and it was not until the middle of January 1945 that Major General J. S. Stevens's division was

complete. MacArthur's operations in the Philippines had a higher priority for the shipping, including vital landing craft; at one point in December 30,000 tonnes of cargo and 2,000 men were riding offshore at anchor, waiting to be unloaded.

Between August and October 1944 the orders given to the 6th Division changed in one important aspect: in August it was clear that the Australians were not to be committed in a major offensive; by October their task was to destroy the enemy forces. General Blamey intended from the beginning to annihilate the Japanese around Aitape and Wewak, rather than merely contain them. The ultimate objective was to take the large Japanese base at Wewak.

Again the Australians had found the Americans less than aggressive towards their enemy. The Japanese XVIII Army, which had been pushed back along the coast after its defeats around Lae and Salamaua, then consisted of about 35,000 men in three understrength divisions. Like their comrades on Bougainville, the Japanese were cut off from resupply, reinforcement and evacuation by sea. Tending their market gardens, and making only occasional forays against the Americans, the Japanese were still sustained by their faith in the Emperor and the discipline of the Imperial Japanese Army.

At first the burden of the operations fell on the 2/6th Cavalry Regiment which, after the Middle East, had been formed into commando units to reconnoitre deep behind the Japanese and bring back vital information. As the commandos probed deeper and deeper they discovered that although the Japanese were numerically strong, they were in poor condition. In January, one patrol operating east of Aitape had come across a hut in which a dozen Japanese lay dead in bed. They bore no wounds, nor obvious signs of sickness. Around the hut the village had been stripped of vegetation. The Japanese had simply died of hunger.

At first the Australian operations were limited to patrolling, but with increasing information and their materiel built up, Stevens planned

COWRA BREAKOUT

As the armies of the Rising Sun reeled back from Allied counter-offensives after late 1942, Japanese prisoners were taken in increasing numbers. More than 5,600 were transported to Australia, where they were imprisoned mostly in three large camps at Cowra and Hay, NSW, and Murchison, Victoria. They joined another 20,000 POWs from Italy and Germany, as well as a few Koreans and Formosans, who were housed in untroubled camps around Australia.

The first signs of discontent appeared at Cowra, a large complex of four camps built in mid-1941. An influx of more than 1,000 Japanese swelled the prison's population, and many of the new inmates were deeply resentful of their imprisonment. They suffered greatly the misery and disgrace of captivity; above all they had been robbed of an honourable death in combat, which their own codes of conduct prided.

They did not complain about their treatment by Australian guards, who scrupulously observed the Geneva Convention concerning the treatment of prisoners. Australian authorities supplied all captives with blankets, clothes and fuel for winter, fresh fish and vegetables on a daily basis and medical attention. But there were early warning signs of a deepening Japanese anxiety. Except for those captured with name tags still on their ragged uniforms, all Japanese POWs gave false names. They refused to communicate with family or friends back home. And, as patients, several struggled against nurses and doctors in desperate efforts to die.

Most of the Japanese prisoners, however, settled down to tend vegetable gardens and play baseball, but many continued to brood on the shame of their captivity. In May 1944, a Korean prisoner forewarned Australian guards of a plan for a mass breakout he had overheard in Camp B. Emergency orders were hastily drawn up and heavier firepower supplied to the garrison. Then on Friday, August 4, the Japanese in Camp B were told that the prisoners were to be separated, with NCOs being transferred to a camp at Hay. If this decision was intended to forestall an escape attempt, it backfired. United as prisoners by a secret death-wish, the Japanese acted swiftly. That day plans were made — orders for the lame to hang themselves were

The body of a young Japanese prisoner swings from a kitchen roof beam in Cowra POW camp after a massed breakout attempt on August 5, 1944. Guards found eight prisoners hanged and 12 incinerated in hut fires.

promptly carried out. At 2 am on Saturday, August 5, 1944, a bugle call signalled an uprising.

Armed with a bizarre array of home-made weapons, 1,100 prisoners hurled themselves at the gates and perimeter of Camp B. They brandished baseball bats, garden tools, and sharpened cutlery, and with blood-curdling yells huts were set ablaze and barbed-wire fences were straddled with blankets and clothes. It was a desperate bid for freedom — or death.

Cornered by the wild mob, the Australian guards opened fire, but many prisoners continued their suici-dal charge. By daybreak the riot was over: four Australians had been killed and four wounded; 231 Japanese were dead and 108 injured. Of the 378 POWs who escaped the camp, 25 killed themselves by hanging, stabbing or jumping under the Cowra train. The rest were rounded up with minimal resistance — no harm was caused to the local population.

An official army inquiry held two days later found that the garrison battalion's self-defensive action during the riot was totally justifiable. The Japanese dead were buried alongside the Australians in the Cowra War Cemetery.

An enemy post is engulfed by fire as an Australian officer demonstrates the deadly power of a flamethrower. The weapon was used with devastating effectiveness to flush out Japanese pillboxes during the Aitape-Wewak campaign.

more ambitious operations, including a two-pronged advance eastwards through the Toricelli Mountains and along the coastal swamps. As they moved forward, the Australians had to battle the climate as well as the Japanese. Torrential rain in January around the Danmap River caused the area to flood. Brigades were washed away and both infantry and commandos suffered drownings.

All the time they were handicapped by the lack of resources. Malarial drugs were in short supply so the incidence of this disease rose alarmingly. At one point Stevens proposed to use an Australian parachute battalion, then training on Queensland's Atherton Tableland, to seize an airstrip which lay in the path of the advance. To deliver that battalion by air required 50 transport C-47 aircraft. Stevens had just one. Still they pressed on. The war diary of the 2/7th Cavalry Squadron noted: "If the ration position doesn't improve, the troops won't be fit to patrol. The signal section is forced to use toilet paper for coding, while all messages outward are on the same kind of paper."

Despite such difficulties, the Australians battled gamely along the coast, taking a series of airfields in late March 1945. Meanwhile, the inland advance also captured an airfield near Maprik able to take heavy transport; the inland force's supply problems were greatly relieved. The Australians, however, were taking regular losses in their small but hard-fought actions, and it was not surprising that the troops of the 6th Division viewed their operations with little enthusiasm. Staff Officer Colonel E. G. Keogh noted, "they had had much experience of war; many of them had fought through the campaigns of the Middle East and the earlier operations in New Guinea. They knew well enough that they were merely mopping up, and they were convinced that no important issue hung upon the result of their labours. In brief, they considered that the enterprise was not worth the exertions they had to make and the price they had to pay."

The 2/4th Battalion's commanding officer, Lieutenant Colonel G. S. Cox, wrote: "It was

noticeable that many of the troops and officers considered that the campaign was not worthwhile, and consequently morale dropped."

But it was the men of the 2/4th Battalion aided by tanks who surged into the outskirts of Wewak and captured the town on May 10. They were joined by the 2/6th Cavalry Regiment commandos, who landed on the beach east of Wewak, and in a few days the large Japanese airfield there was in Allied hands. Many of the Japanese troops who had been in the area had, by now, escaped into the interior, but still they had lost more than 5,000 killed. For the Australians, however, it was another useless and futile operation which had cost them more than 450 killed.

On New Britain, Major General A. H. Ramsay adopted a different approach from that of the commanders on Bougainville and Aitape. His 5th Division, suffering the same problems of inadequate supplies and non-existent air support, and heavily outnumbered by the defenders, ran almost a perfect containment operation. The problems faced by Ramsay were similar to those faced by Savige and Stevens, but the 5th Division commander made it clear to his subordinates that large-scale offensives were simply not worth the risk.

Most of the 38,000 Japanese troops on New Britain were around Rabaul. Had they taken the offensive against the Australians, it is more than likely that Ramsay's men would have been in serious trouble. But the policy of containment worked well; the Japanese around Rabaul were unable to move and the 5th Division achieved its aim without suffering many casualties.

At the height of operations on Bougainville, around Aitape and Wewak, and on New Britain, the mopping-up campaigns were seriously questioned in Australia. Originally Australians had very little information about the fighting because censorship imposed by MacArthur's headquarters prevented war correspondents reporting that Australian troops had taken over from the Americans. In January 1945 the *Canberra Times* asked: "Would anyone knowing the whereabouts of Australian soldiers in action in the South West Pacific Area please communicate at once with the Australian Government?" On the very same day, however, the newspapers reported the fact that the 5th Division landings had taken place on New Britain three months earlier. The censorship had been totally unnecessary.

With the news now out in the open, the operations themselves came under discussion in Parliament. Robert Menzies, then leading a resurgent Liberal Party in opposition, started a debate in which the tasks given to the Australian troops came under intense scrutiny. Menzies was concerned that the Australians had not been given "a first-class strategic objective" and that the latest operations were a waste of fine Australian soldiers. The Opposition Leader wanted the Australian troops to be made available to British commanders in proposed operations for the recapture of Singapore and Malaya. Menzies asked, "Are we to use our forces primarily for doing what I call 'mopping up operations' in by-passed areas, or should they be used as an integral portion of a British army to deliver those countries in the Far East which have been overrun by Japan?"

In the Government's reply, the External Affairs Minister, Dr Evatt, said the operations had been "determined" by General MacArthur, and that no role in this theatre was secondary. Evatt's statements were simply wrong; the Australian Government was trying to defuse the issue as best it could. Blamey, too, was coming under considerable pressure. One politician claimed in the debate that the army was "seething with dissatisfaction". The Australian general now entered the debate personally in a national broadcast on April 15, describing his parliamentary critics as "amateurs" not concerned about the effect their publicly aired views might be having on the morale of the troops. Blamey's speech, however, was seen as self-justification. One newspaper described it as an "ill-tempered, unseemly outburst".

The Government and especially Prime Minister John Curtin, who was seriously ill, were coming under increasing pressure. He quoted to Parliament a letter he had received from MacArthur in which the American general stated that the local Australian commanders had "considerable freedom of action as to methods employed." But Curtin also sought Blamey's reasons for taking the offensive in the mopping-up campaigns. Blamey replied in a detailed memorandum, but by now Curtin, who was his main political supporter, was away from Parliament ill. The acting Prime Minister, Ben Chifley, was more sceptical about the Australian general and, as well, he had a letter from MacArthur who wrote, "I and my head-quarters never favoured (the islands operation), and while its execution had been successful and 147

Saturated and exhausted, Australian sappers of 2/13th Field Company watch their explosive charges blow gaps in enemy beach obstacles at Tarakan. Wading chest-deep in mud, and under fire, sappers cleared the beaches without casualties.

efficient in every way, I regard its initiation as having been unnecessary and inadvisable."

MacArthur's focus was obviously on operations closer to Japan; he was no longer interested in what was happening in the islands to Australia's near north. But he did take an interest in Borneo. Japan had targeted Borneo in its initial South-East Asian grab because of its raw materials, especially oil, and its strategic proximity to Malaya and the East Indies. Now MacArthur argued that the retaking of Borneo would cut Japan's supply of oil and add to the Allies' stocks for later operations. It was a spurious case: Japan had already been cut off from its oil by American submarines, and it was unlikely that fuel could be turned on for the Allies for at least a year. MacArthur also saw Borneo as an opportunity to restore British and Dutch rule in the area, as well as a convenient channel ·to occupy Australian troops and thus diffuse the raging criticism over their misuse.

The Australian Government had requested an increased role for its AIF soldiers, some of whom had not taken part in the war since 1943. MacArthur passed on the request to the American Joint Chiefs of Staff, suggesting that "the postponement for many months of employment of Australian troops will produce grave repercussions with the Australian Government and people."

However, when Chifley mooted after the end of the war in Europe in May that he might withdraw one of the Australian divisions suggested for the Borneo campaign, the 7th, MacArthur was furious, claiming that the formation was essential for the operation's success. MacArthur was clearly hedging his bets, and not for the first time intimidating the Australian politicians.

The American general wanted the Australian troops for their obvious fighting qualities, particularly the 7th and 9th Divisions which now had valuable amphibious experience. But while MacArthur was happy to have the fighting men, he was unwilling to share any limelight with a competing general; he did not want any Australian formation headquarters

higher than a corps. Ironically, it was Blamey who was bypassed, because MacArthur decided to directly command the Australians himself, with the I Australian Corps being headed by Lieutenant General Leslie Morshead. There was no room for an Australian operational commander between MacArthur and Morshead.

Known to the troops as "Ming the Merciless" after a contemporary cartoon character, Morshead had commanded the 9th Division at Tobruk and El Alamein. Now he was responsible for three major landings at Tarakan, Brunei Bay and at Balikpapan before major clearing operations got underway in Borneo. Codenamed "Oboe", these missions involved the 7th Division capturing Balikpapan, and the 9th Division less its 26th Brigade attacking Brunei Bay. The 26th Brigade, reinforced with two pioneer battalions, a commando squadron, a squadron of tanks and an anti-aircraft regiment, was to land at Tarakan island, the first of the Australians' objectives, to provide airfields and support for the major attacks onto Borneo. A commando squadron and a battery of guns were landed first on a tiny island off the coast of Tarakan. Their task was to protect the engineers busily demolishing the obstacles placed by the Japanese on the landing beaches.

Then, on May 1, the assault on Tarakan island began. The weaponry used was immense: supporting the three battalions were two cruisers, six destroyers and the battery on the small island. The leading waves hit the beaches to the southwest of Tarakan township, met no opposition and quickly pushed inland. One battalion, however, met spirited opposition on heights overlooking the beaches, and it took five days to force back the defenders and take the town and airfield, five kilometres to the north. Pockets of stubborn resistance, however, remained in hills just north of the town, and throughout May Australian forces, including the 2/48th Battalion, saw vicious close-in fighting against dug-in Japanese units.

The Australians threw everything they had at the enemy strongholds, including regular aerial

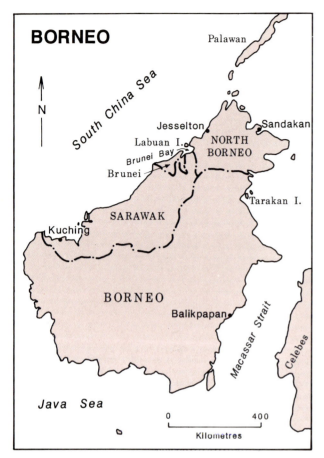

BORNEO

Palawan

South China Sea

N

Jesselton

Labuan I.

Brunei Bay

Brunei

NORTH BORNEO

Sandakan

SARAWAK

Kuching

Tarakan I.

BORNEO

Balikpapan

Macassar Strait

Celebes

Java Sea

0   400

Kilometres

In the last months of the war, major Australian operations at Tarakan, Labuan, Brunei Bay and Balikpapan isolated small pockets of Japanese resistance.

His battalion was stunned at the loss, its diarist writing that "he had become a legend, and an inspiration to the whole unit. In what proved to be his last campaign he fought as ever with utmost courage and devotion to duty." His death was amongst a casualty toll of close to 900 Australians and 1,500 Japanese killed.

And, in the end, the battle for Tarakan was a frustration for all: the very airfield the commanders had wanted was inoperable because the Japanese had demolished it beyond repair in time for Australia's following actions at Brunei and Balikpapan.

Nonetheless, the next phase went ahead at Brunei Bay and Labuan Island, which commanded both the northern and southern entrances to the bay. Three landings on separate beaches were planned so well that they occurred within four minutes of each other on June 10, 1945. The landing craft disengaged themselves from the mother ships and ran smoothly into the shore, protected all the time by air cover from American carriers and by a massive preliminary bombardment. If there were Japanese forces on the beaches they soon withdrew, for no major opposition was struck by the Australians who had the town of Brunei secure on the first day. Then the Diggers settled down to a difficult patrolling war, using native boats on the many streams and waterways.

The heaviest fighting of this campaign was to be found at Balikpapan, but again the Australian troops were extremely well equipped, and after such long periods of inactivity they were anxious to get back into the fight. Captain Malcolm Uren of the 2/16th Battalion considered that this was a new kind of war. There was, he said, "No probing for the unseen enemy, no wondering about the kind of terrain, no doubts about air support or supplies, no lack of equipment and no fugitive feeling about being out on their own. Here was a minutely planned attack in appropriate numbers on an objective the strength of which could be reasonably well assessed."

For 20 days before the Balikpapan landings, U.S. and Australian aircraft pounded the

and artillery bombardment as well as napalm. The Japanese stood fast on a series of knolls, but now two companies of the 2/48th went in after them in the fading light of dusk on May 22. Amongst the attackers was Lieutenant Tom "Diver" Derrick's platoon, who courageously breached a saddle joining two heavily defended knolls. During the dark night that followed, no further progress could be made, and in the morning the Japanese hit back. In the light of day, Derrick's platoon area was found to be directly under an enemy bunker, and the Japanese there quickly seized the advantage and overpowered the Diggers. The vicious hand-to-hand fighting was as brutal as any engagement Derrick and his men had encountered — in Tobruk, El Alamein, Lae, Finschhafen, and at Sattelberg, where the "Diver" had earned his Victoria Cross. Now, Derrick was hit in the stomach and thigh, but he continued to give orders for some hours until the Australians were forced to pull back, carrying their casualties with them. Lieutenant Derrick did

150   not survive his wounds.

Within days of successful amphibious assaults on Labuan island and Brunei, soldiers of 2/32nd Battalion disembark from an American landing craft on mainland North Borneo in June 1945.

beaches. Then, as the Australians waited off shore in their landing craft, warships and rocket barges added their massive firepower to the targets. "Never before had the Australians seen such destructive forces let loose by their side," wrote Uren. "The air and the sea shook and reverberated to the crashing discharge of hundreds of naval guns. Salvo after salvo screamed overhead; great gouts of flame, dirt and smoke spewed from the river and tortured earth. Whole buildings and trees were tossed grotesquely in the air, to fall back shapeless and shuddering. All the time the Japanese guns continued firing but without much effect. The airforce added its quota to the inferno until it seemed nothing could possibly live on or near those belted beaches."

The firepower available to the Australians was awesome. One company of the 2/16th Battalion, with a task of landing first on the beach at Balikpapan, had in support a squadron

of divebombers from an American aircraft carrier, an American cruiser, a battery of artillery, four Vickers machine-guns from an Australian machine-gun battalion, and four 4.2 inch mortars. As well, the company commander had under his command half the battalion's 3-inch mortars and half the medium machine-guns. "Never were the troops so well briefed for the task in hand," Uren wrote. "Every man knew exactly the job to be done, both from the 'bigger picture' and his own individual task. Every man knew the ground as though he had lived there for weeks, and it was a grand tribute to the planning of the action that the terrain was exactly as was expected."

The immense pounding left some landmarks almost unrecognisable. Once the battalion was ashore, it found the assembly area more by a sense of direction than anything else. Again at Balikpapan, as with the earlier landings, there was little opposition on the beaches themselves 151

An American manned landing ship carrying 7th Australian Division troops drops its ramps at Balikpapan beachhead on July 1, 1945. Smoke from a burning oil refinery darkens the sky over the foreshore, devastated by Allied bombardment.

but on July 1, 1945, as the 21st Brigade pushed inland it met fierce Japanese defenders on the far side of the Batakan Ketjil River. Naval guns were now brought to bear on the enemy, directed by a navy gunnery officer ashore with the soldiers, and by that afternoon the Japanese defences were in Australian hands.

Through July the Australians continued to meet opposition as they pursued the withdrawing Japanese. Their enemy, although poorly supplied, sick and emaciated, still fought with skill and determination, especially when cornered. Always, the Australians had superior firepower; for one battalion attack on a 300 metres by 200 metres Japanese rearguard position, 8,000 rounds were fired. Another time a similarly sized enemy group was attacked first by artillery, then by aircraft and finally by tanks before the infantry went in with rifles and bayonets. The superiority in firepower, the massive logistical support, and the freshness of the Australian troops soon proved too strong. By the middle of July 1945, serious Japanese opposition ceased to exist. From then until the end of the war a month later, the Australians confined themselves to patrolling activity.

The war in Borneo, as on Bougainville and around Aitape-Wewak, petered out in the last few months. There were no great battalion attacks, just the relentless grind of patrolling. For all the technical skill and expertise of the operations in Borneo, they were as unnecessary as their counterparts further to the south. The war had moved on, closer to Japan, even before the first Australian soldier set foot on Borneo. For all of MacArthur's island-hopping techniques, here were garrisons that should have been bypassed. Instead, they were fought over

Gunners of the 2/4th Field Regiment lob shells into enemy positions at Balikpapan. Forced to withdraw after a tremendous coastal barrage, the Japanese quickly re-established defences outside the township and fought back bitterly.

and Australian casualties sustained: 225 killed and 669 wounded at Tarakan; 114 killed or died of wounds in north Borneo; and 229 killed and 634 wounded at Balikpapan.

While the Australians fought on in Borneo, as well as on the islands closer to home, American forces were incurring heavy losses just south of Japan itself, on Iwo Jima and Okinawa islands, as enemy forces increasingly fought to the death to save their country's pride and fast-crumbling empire. During July heavy U.S. bombers increased their devastation of major cities on Japan's home islands, preparing for an expected landing of ground troops.

Admiral Chester Nimitz was fully aware that the fighting ahead would be difficult. ''We must be prepared to accept heavy casualties whenever we invade Japan,'' he said. Such risks, however, were obviously far too daunting

for America's leaders, who decided instead to drop an atomic bomb on the Japanese city of Hiroshima on August 6, and another on Nagasaki on August 9. The next day, Japan's Emperor agreed to sue for peace, and on August 15 Japan accepted the Allies' surrender terms.

For the thousands of servicemen still in the Pacific theatre when the bombs dropped, there was an overpowering sense of relief that the war was now over. Each success had come for them at a huge price. There had been no great pursuit, no sudden crumbling of the defences. The war had ended for many of them with a bang — and a whimper. On Borneo, the 2/16th's Captain Uren recalled the awful newsflash: ''We had had a secret weapon — and a more terrible weapon than anyone had guessed. Suddenly, after all the years of bitter travail, there was time for introspection.''

The Pacific campaign had been Australia's closest war — the only time in its history of fighting other peoples' wars that the enemy actually got to the front door. Yet it was those bitter months of late 1942, when the Japanese had to be pushed back across the Kokoda Track and blasted out of their defences in northern Papua, that invite attention. Those campaigns were fought on the military equivalent of a shoestring, nonetheless Australian soldiers developed an enviable expertise in jungle warfare. The lessons they had learned at such cost in Malaya, then in Papua and New Guinea, were passed on to young soldiers. The army set up the Jungle Training Centre at Canungra in the Gold Coast hinterland, where it trained men for the Pacific war. They learned to live in appalling conditions in tropical jungles, with the feeling of always being tired, sick and hungry, and of clothes and equipment rotting from the damp. They learned to care for their weapons, particularly the trusty Owen gun, developed in Australia and which, it was demonstrated, fired even after being dropped in mud.

In Papua the Australians had met the Japanese and turned them back. This was their major contribution, followed by a supreme effort that took some years to clear the Japanese out of New Guinea. The conduct of the war from 1944 by Australian politicians and generals was, however, questionable, and certainly an anti-climax. Still, through it all, the Australian soldier kept on at his job. His remarkable good humour, his comradeship, his belief in his own competence and those of his mates around him, saw him through. It saddened the veterans when they saw one of their number killed towards the end of the war. Lieutenant Tom "Diver" Derrick was one of them. He had won a Distinguished Combat Medal in the desert, and a Victoria Cross in New Guinea. There were many in the AIF who believed that Tom Derrick had done his bit. But then, so had they all, the recognised and the unsung heroes alike.

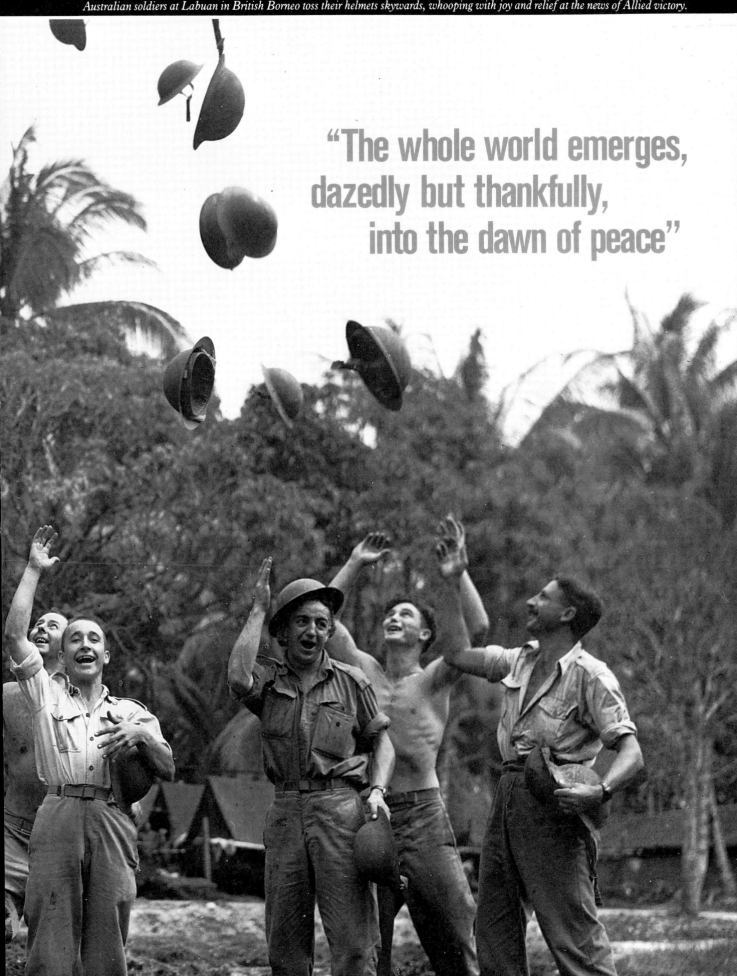

Australian soldiers at Labuan in British Borneo toss their helmets skywards, whooping with joy and relief at the news of Allied victory.

"The whole world emerges, dazedly but thankfully, into the dawn of peace"

WAR'S EPILOGUE

At 9.30 am on August 15, 1945, Australian Prime Minister Ben Chifley broadcast to the nation that the Japanese had accepted the Allies' surrender terms. He declared that day and the next public holidays. The announcement was greeted with great fanfare; the *Sydney Morning Herald* proclaimed: "The whole world emerges, dazedly but thankfully, into the dawn of peace." Delirium broke out with jubilant crowds dancing, singing and waving flags in the streets of every Australian town and city.

Many soldiers still far from home were less euphoric. Lieutenant Clive Edwards, stationed in Morotai, wrote to his father: "It's strange to think of it as being really all over. When the news went through it was an anticlimax. We will forgo our celebration until we can have a family reunion with all of us together." He was not discharged until December 1945.

Repatriation of troops was slow because of the lack of shipping. An interim army was also set up to occupy and police enemy territories. Like many, Lieutenant Ford McKernan RAN remained suspicious of the enemy, and he wrote home: "The war is still very long-winded in the finishing off and we don't trust them any too far."

After a historic surrender ceremony in Tokyo Bay on September 2, 1945, Japanese commanders in the field received orders to lay down their arms. During that month Australian Army commanders then accepted the surrender of Japanese forces in areas where Australians had fought, and the Japanese were generally cooperative in giving up their arms and safely delivering POWs and internees. Australian military courts throughout South-East Asia and in Darwin went on to hold 296 war-crimes trials, in which 924 Japanese were charged; 148 were hanged and 496 imprisoned.

Most Australian troops returned home by mid-1946. Despite government job-training and land-selection schemes, many soldiers found readjustment to civilian life difficult. They faced estranged families, a housing crisis, and for many, unrewarding jobs. They lived with injuries and distressing memories, but at least they lived — in a world no longer at war.

A Japanese soldier bows his head in humble salute to a truckload of Australian and

Dutch troops on Ceram island in October 1945. Japanese II Army troops on Ceram were allowed to retain limited arms to maintain law and order.

During victory celebrations in Melbourne on VJ (Victory Japan) Day, a returned Digger cheers from the excited crowd.

A Japanese prisoner of war on Guam weeps to hear his Emperor's broadcast announcing Japan's unconditional surrender.

161

In a spontaneous and nationwide bout of peace delirium, an exuberant crowd throngs Martin Place in Sydney on August 15, 1945. People danced in

conga lines and Hokey Pokey rings, waved Union Jacks and threw torn paper confetti to celebrate the end of what had been a seemingly endless war.

BIBLIOGRAPHY

Andrews, Michael. *Australia and the Pacific.* Sydney: Dreamweaver Books, 1985

Austin, Victor. *To Kokoda and Beyond.* Melbourne: Melbourne University Press, 1988

Bell, R.J. *Unequal Allies.* Melbourne: Melbourne University Press, 1977

Brigg, Stan and Les. *The 36th Australian Infantry Battalion.* Sydney: Angus & Robertson, 1967

Chrystal, Cecil anor. *White Over Green, The History of the 2/4th Battalion.* Sydney: Angus & Robertson, 1963

Clift, Ken. *War Dance. The History of the 2/3rd Battalion.* Sydney: Privately published, 1980

Costello, John. *The Pacific War.* London: Collins, 1981

Cranston, Fred. *"Always Faithful", The History of the 49th Battalion.* Brisbane: Boolarong, 1983

Crooks, William. *The Footsoldiers.* Sydney: Printcraft Press Pty Ltd, 1971

Dexter, David. *The New Guinea Offensives.* Canberra: Australian War Memorial, 1961

Farquhar, Murray. *Derrick VC.* Adelaide: Rigby, 1982

Gill, G.H. *Royal Australian Navy, 1939-1942.* Sydney: Collins, Australian War Memorial, 1985

—. *Royal Australian Navy, 1942-1945.* Sydney: Collins, Australian War Memorial, 1985

Harrison-Ford, Carl. (ed.) *Fighting Words.* Melbourne: Lothian Publishing Co., 1986

Hay, Sir David. *Nothing Over Us, The History of the 2/6th Battalion.* Canberra: Australian War Memorial, 1984

Hetherington, John. *Blamey, Controversial Soldier.* Canberra: Australian War Memorial, 1973

Hopkins, Major General R.N.L. *Australian Armour.* Canberra: Australian War Memorial, 1978

Horner, D.M. *Crisis of Command.* Canberra: ANU Press, 1978

—. *High Command.* Sydney: Allen & Unwin, 1982

—. (ed.) *The Commanders Australian Military Leadership in the Twentieth Century.* Sydney: Allen & Unwin, 1974

James, D.C. *The Years of MacArthur, Volume II, 1941-45.* Boston: Houghton Mifflin, 1975

Johnston, G.H. *New Guinea Diary.* Sydney: Angus & Robertson, 1944

—. *War Diary 1942.* Sydney: Collins, 1984

Keogh, E.G. *The South West Pacific 1941-45.* Melbourne: Grayflower, 1963

Lodge, Brett. *The Fall of General Gordon Bennett.* Sydney: Allen & Unwin, 1986

Long, Gavin. *The Six Years War.* Canberra: Australian War Memorial

MacArthur, Douglas. *Reminiscences.* New York: Heinemann, 1964

Mathews, Russel. *Militia Battalion At War. The History of the 58th/59th Battalion.* Sydney: 1961

Mayo, Linda. *Bloody Buna.* New York: Doubleday, 1974

McCarthy, Dudley. *South West Pacific Area — Kokoda to Wau.* Canberra: Australian War Memorial, 1959

McKernan, Michael. *All In!.* Melbourne: Nelson, 1983

McKinlay, Brian. *Australia 1942 — End of Innocence.* Sydney: Collins, 1985

Milner, S.B. *Victory in Papua.* Washington Office of the Chief of Military History, U.S. Army, 1957

Morison, S.E. *The Two Ocean War.* Boston: Little Brown & Co, 1963

Odgers, George. *The Royal Australian Air Force — An Illustrated History.* Brookvale: Child & Henry Publishing, 1984

—. *The Royal Australian Navy — An Illustrated History.* Brookvale: Child & Henry Publishing, 1984

—. *Air War Against Japan 1943-1945.* Canberra: Australian War Memorial, 1968

Paull, Raymond. *Retreat from Kokoda.* Melbourne: Heinemann, 1958

Reader's Digest. *Illustrated Story of World War II.* Sydney: Reader's Digest, 1970

Reischauer, E.O. & A.M. Craig. *Japan Tradition and Transformation.* Sydney: Allen & Unwin, 1985

Robertson, John. *Australia at War, 1939-1945.* Melbourne: Heinemann, 1981

Robertson, John and John McCarthy. *Australian War Strategy 1939-1945, A Documentary History.* Brisbane: University of Queensland Press, 1985

Rolleston, Frank. *Not a Conquering Hero.* Mackay: Privately published, 1983

Simson, Ivan. *Singapore — Too Little, Too Late.* London: Lee Cooper, 1970

Steward, H.D. *Recollections of a Regimental Medical Officer.* Melbourne: Melbourne University Press, 1983

Storry, Richard. *A History of Modern Japan.* Middlesex: Penguin, 1982

Stuart, Lurline and Josie Arnold. *Letters Home 1939-1945.* Sydney: Collins, 1987

Uren, Malcolm. *A Thousand Men At War, The Story of the 2/16th Battalion.* Melbourne: 1959

White, Osmar. *Green Armour.* Sydney: Angus & Robertson, 1946

Wigmore, Lionel. *The Japanese Thrust.* Canberra: Australian War Memorial, 1957

ACKNOWLEDGEMENTS

For their help in the publication of this book, the author and publishers wish to thank the staff of the Australian War Memorial, Canberra, especially Dr Michael McKernan, Bill Fogarty, Ian Affleck, George Imashev, Matthew Woodhead, Anthony Rudniki, Vincent Trundle, Raeburn Trindall, Dina Junkermann, Joyce Bradley, Angela Wynants, Nancy Tinguy, Jeanne Klovdahl and Jean McAuslen. We would also like to thank Mihri Tansley, Flexigraphics, Sally Olive, the United Service Institution of NSW Library, Kathleen Reidy, Andrew Chalk, Neil McDonald, Group Captain Clive Caldwell, Roger Scott, Annette Macarthur Onslow, George Edwards, Major McGregor and Tom Rose of the Central Army Records Office and the 2/3rd Independent Company's Arthur Little, Bernard Casey and Arthur Bazely.

PICTURE CREDITS

Credits from left to right are separated by semi-colons, from top to bottom by oblique strokes. AWM = Australian War Memorial, Canberra. IWM = Imperial War Museum, London.

COVER and Page 1: AWM 13645.

STRUGGLE FOR PAPUA. 6: AWM Art Dept. 26387. 8, 9: Map by Flexigraphics. 10, 11: AWM Pictorial History of Australia at War Vol 3, Page 125 (bottom). 12, 13: Mainichi Shimbun. 14: AWM 26727. 15: AWM 13155; AWM 13266. 17: AWM 13620. 18, 19: AWM 26837; AWM 27054; AWM 13705 / AWM Map Section. 20: AWM 13287. 21: AWM 69246. 22, 23: AWM 27004. 25: AWM 13002. 26: AWM 13405 / AWM 18197. 27: AWM 13598. 29: AWM 26852. 30: AWM 26582. 31: AWM 27053. 32: AWM 13420. 33: AWM 27025. 35: AWM 27081. 37: AWM 14659. 38: AWM 52620. 40, 41: AWM 13572. 42: AWM 13621. 44: AWM 13755.

ANGELS OF WAR. 46, 47: National Library of Australia, Canberra. 48: AWM 16727. 49: AWM 13600. 50: AWM 64243. 51: AWM 17043. 52, 53: AWM 93223.

THE BEACHHEAD BATTLES. 54: AWM Art Dept. 26411. 56: Map by Flexigraphics. 59: AWM 13736. 61: Courtesy Fairfax Picture Library 41-409A. 62: AWM 136375 / AWM 65322. 63: Courtesy Herald and Weekly Times Limited / AWM 11544. 64: AWM 57571. 65: AWM 13992. 67: Courtesy Hugh Clarke, AWM 13880. 68: AWM 13877. 70, 71: Pictorial History of Australia at War 1939-1945, Vol 3, Page 208 (top). 72: AWM 13930. 73: AWM 14037. 74, 75: Courtesy Hugh Clarke, AWM 14005. 76: AWM 14002. 77: IWM OEM4356. 78, 79: AWM 14234.

PROPAGANDA WAR. 81-89: AWM Printed Collection, Leaflet Collection.

GAINING GROUND IN NEW GUINEA. 90: AWM Art Dept. 26417. 92: AWM 151947. 93: Map by Flexigraphics. 95: AWM 14372. 96: AWM 76134. 98, 99: AWM 15227. 100: AWM 15323. 101: AWM 15318. 102: AWM 15515.

COMBAT CAMERA. 104, 105: AWM P928/08/05. 106: AWM 44129. 107: AWM 127971. 108: AWM 127981. 109: AWM 127980 / AWM P928/08/07. 110, 111: AWM 127986.

TAKING THE HUON PENINSULA. 112: AWM Art Dept. 26388. 114: Map by Flexigraphics. 115: AWM 68593. 116, 117: AWM 100546. 119: AWM 15929. 120, 121: AWM 57461. 122: AWM 16205. 123: AWM 16214. 125: AWM 70300. 126: AWM 15955. 127: AWM 16983. 128: AWM 64260.

WINNING THE AIR WAR. 130, 131: AWM 127624. 132: AWM 44535. 133: National Library of Australia, Canberra. 134, 135: AWM 61955; AWM 8314; AWM OG1970 / AWM OG1933. 136, 137: AWM OG1343.

MOPPING UP. 138: AWM Art Dept. 26925. 140: Map by Flexigraphics. 141: AWM 17904. 143: AWM 18392. 145: Courtesy Hugh Clarke, AWM 44170. 146: AWM 18407. 148: AWM 90907. 150: Map by Flexigraphics. 151: AWM 18680. 152: AWM 128283. 153: AWM 19437. 154: Courtesy Hugh Clarke.

VICTORY. 156, 157: AWM OG3235A. 158, 159: AWM 121109. 160: AWM 181808. 161: AWM P444/ /98. 162, 163: AWM 113847.

Every effort has been made to contact and acknowledge owners of copyright in illustrative material used in this book. In the case of an omission, holders of copyright are invited to contact:

John Ferguson Publishers
100 Kippax St.
Surry Hills, N.S.W.
2010.

PICTURE ESSAY QUOTES

ANGELS OF WAR: "May the mothers of Australia, when they offer up a prayer, mention those impromptu angels with their fuzzy wuzzy hair." Sapper H. Beros.

COMBAT CAMERA: "My task was to convey the moment of truth when a soldier charges to kill or be killed." Damien Parer.

WINNING THE AIR WAR: "Our air boys are right on top and giving them hell." Lieutenant Colonel E. Macarthur Onslow.

VICTORY: "The whole world emerges, dazedly but thankfully, into the dawn of peace." *Sydney Morning Herald*, 16 August 1945.

INDEX

*Numerals in italics indicate an
illustration of the subject mentioned.*